# Eternal Sunshine
## of the Spotless Mind

# Eternal Sunshine
## of the Spotless Mind

### Love, Loss, and
### the Fade to White

### (Auteur)

---

## Maia Wyman

New York, NY

Copyright © 2025 by Vashti Maia Wyman.
All rights reserved.

This book is memoir. It reflects the author's present recollections of experiences over time.

No part of this book may be used or reproduced in any manner without written permission of the publisher. Please direct inquiries to:

Ig Publishing
Box 2547
New York, NY 10163
www.igpub.com

ISBN: 978-1-63246-173-5

PRINTED IN THE UNITED STATES OF AMERICA

"He who learns must suffer. And even in our sleep, pain that cannot forget falls drop by drop upon the heart, and in our own despair, against our will, comes wisdom to us by the awful grace of god."

—*Agamemnon l. 176*

## Introduction

In the weeks leading up to my breakup, I slept a meager three hours a night. There was a thickness in the air that knew the planes of my life were about to shift, and it was keeping me awake. The night it happened, I slept next to my mother. She awoke to my frustrated sobs around four in the morning, and placed a warm hand on my cheek. We lay there in silence for about an hour, until I finally fell asleep. The emotions came crashing back when I opened my eyes a couple hours later. I took the day off work, dragged myself home, and turned on *Eternal Sunshine of the Spotless Mind.*

I fell in love five years ago. Having never been in love before, I readily threw myself into this relationship. He and I tumbled head-first into things—spendings days at a time at each other's apartments, sending long, saccharine Facebook messages when one of us left the city for a couple days, and opening up in the wee hours of the morning about our family lives, past relationships, and undisclosed desires. This came to an abrupt halt when we were forced to enter a ten-month period of long distance, just three short months into our romance. It was during this time that I watched *Eternal Sunshine* on repeat.

Michel Gondry's enigmatic sci-fi romance about a couple, Joel and Clementine, who attempt to erase each other from memory, was so powerful and tender that you could feel their yearning through the screen. For me, it was the filmic embodiment of love. Our love was trapped within Facetime calls and iMessages, and the tenuous fracture of a three-hour time difference was threatening to run it off course. So my ritual viewings of *Eternal Sunshine* allowed me to replicate that elusive, exhilarating feeling while I waited for him to move back home.

Somehow, five years later and in the throes of a breakup from that same relationship, I was watching it again.

It's very strange that a film could fulfill two opposing needs. I needed *Eternal Sunshine* to remind me of what love felt like—that feeling that you are two atoms floating in space, compulsively drifting towards one another despite what lies between you. I also needed *Eternal Sunshine* to allow me to sit in my own unfathomable sadness. Already, taking the day off of work felt melodramatic, as did blubbering to my friends. But my emotions were there. I needed the film to tell me that what I was experiencing was real loss. That a facet of my soul had been severed and that, like any other loss, I would need to grieve it. I would need to grieve him, even though we were texting every day. My friends were seeing him out on the street or at concerts, looking glum and uncomfortable. I could call him at any time and ask him to come over. By all accounts he was still there, but I needed to grieve. And in order to do that, I needed to forget him.

*Eternal Sunshine of the Spotless Mind* came out in 2004. It was directed by Gondry and written by Charlie Kaufman, a duo of eccentrics whose whimsical works are often tinged by darkness. It stars Jim Carrey as Joel and Kate Winslet as Clementine—doing an opposites act. Carrey was believed to be too goofy for the role, Winslet too serious. It also features a remarkable cast of supporting actors, Kirsten Dunst, Elijah Wood, Mark Ruffalo, and Tom Wilkinson. The film takes place in a heightened version of our own world—the streets are gray, cars are dirty, and living rooms are cluttered. But it's a world where Joel and Clementine, unable to deal with the pain of their breakup, can actually undergo a memory-removal process in the drab office of a firm called Lacuna Inc. The operation is performed by Dr. Howard Mierzwiak, played by Wilkinson, and his team of young technicians—Stan, played by Ruffalo, and Patrick, played by Wood. There's also a receptionist named Mary, who runs the daily operations of the firm, played by Dunst.

The film begins on a cold Valentine's Day morning. We meet Joel as he awakes, disoriented, on a pull-out bed in his cluttered Yonkers, New York apartment. He groggily boards a train to Montauk, revealing to the viewer in voiceover that he ditched work that day. Why? He does not know. Why he is on a train to Montauk, he does not know either. He goes to the beach, where he sees a woman with blue hair and tells himself, "If only I could meet someone new." He sees the woman again at a diner a short while later, and she's revealed to be Clementine. The two get to talking on the train back to New York, and while Joel finds Clementine a bit irritating, he feels endeared to her. They spend the rest of the day and night together. But when Joel drives Clementine home so she can grab her toothbrush and resume hanging out, a young man comes up to his car and asks him what he's doing there, leaving Joel mystified.

We then cut to nighttime. Joel is sobbing in his car as the title sequence rolls. Names in a childlike font crumble just as soon as they appear, as Beck's "Everybody's Gotta Learn Sometime" plays moodily overtop. Joel stumbles into his place looking bewildered, as two young men in a van pull up to the house. He takes some pills from an envelope marked "Lacuna Inc." and passes out on the floor as one of the men quips disinterestedly, "Showtime at the Apollo…" The scene cuts again and we're with an anguished Joel in the apartment of his friends, a bickering couple. He laments that he and Clementine got into a fight. When he went to patch things over at the bookstore, her place of work, she didn't seem to know who he was. There was also a strange man with her, acting very familiar. The friends, sympathetic, show him the following letter, signed Lacuna Inc.:

Dear Mr. and Mrs. Eakin,

Clementine Kruczynski has had Joel Barish erased from her memory. Please never mention their relationship to her again.

Thank you.

Here, Joel and Clementine's interaction in Montauk appears to be their first ever meeting, and that the events which follow it take place after their relationship has ended.

But through the course of the movie, Joel and Clementine's romance and subsequent falling out is told to us through distorted memories, as well as present events. It's through this journey we learn that soon after he receives the letter, Joel decides to remove his own memory as well. And that, while the two had met for the first time in Montauk two years earlier, this had all happened before we meet them at the beginning of the film.

Running in tandem with this is a subplot centred on the Lacuna staff members. The technicians are particularly careless with their work on Joel, as he lies unconscious on his bed, a mess of gadgets strapped to his head. Stan, the head technician, is distracted because Mary, his quasi-girlfriend, has shown up looking for a good time. Patrick, Stan's assistant and a decidedly weaselly character, is consumed by his infatuation for a rapidly unravelling Clementine. (He was the strange man who knocked on Joel's car window. He was also the strange man from the bookstore.) Having fallen "in love" with her as she lay unconscious during her own procedure, Patrick takes advantage of her newly erased memory and uses information about her past relationship to pursue one with her himself. Mary is also distracted by a clandestine infatuation for a married Dr. Mierzwiak—when he comes to oversee Joel's operation after something goes awry, she makes a move on him. We then learn that she and Dr. Mierzwiak previously had an affair, but that Mary had her memory removed to overcome her unrequited love for him. Upon finding out about her memory removal, she returns all of Lacuna's files back to their patients, deeming the process unethical.

This is how Joel and Clementine, during the car ride back to Joel's apartment, hazily discover that they have actually dated before. However, it is ambiguous if the technicians' botching of the process led Joel and Clementine to find each other again, or if it was fate. In my reading, their reconnection is not achieved by happenstance, but by the fortitude of Joel's and Clementine's love for one another. The two dart in and out of his crumbling memories together, and try their best to resist erasure. It's unclear at the end of the film whether Clementine's final plea, "Meet me in Montauk" survives in Joel's unconscious or whether their connection is so unbreakable that they would be compelled to each other no matter what.

The experience of watching *Eternal Sunshine* is an embodied one, in that it actually makes you feel like you are about to slip into a blissful sleep. While the film has often been referred to as "sci-fi", there is a lived-in quality to the mise-en-scène which makes this easy to overlook. By stitching the more absurd elements of the story into banal settings, Gondry achieves a cerebral viewing experience that makes *Eternal Sunshine* oddly soothing to view. This is the reason I chose to watch it the day after my breakup. For myself, and I'm sure many others, *Eternal Sunshine* is deeply therapeutic. It knows the abject pain of romantic loss, but it does not let you push that pain away. Instead, it soothes your pain by walking you through the emotions of grief, letting you off at the end not fully whole, but slightly less tortured. I was not sleeping during that time, but *Eternal Sunshine* posed as sleep. It gently lulled me into confronting all my horrible, beautiful memories and gave me the levity I needed so badly. These words—gentle, horrible, confronting, and beautiful—are contradictory yet they all ring true here. Because *Eternal Sunshine* so deftly evades genre, it's able to leave you with complicated and contrasting feelings.

## One: Romantic Grief

Experts have long acknowledged psychological parallels in the wake of both death and romantic failure. In the event of a breakup, sufferers have been shown to have trouble remembering things, experience a loss of purpose, and find it difficult to focus on daily tasks. They may also feel anger, panic, sadness, emotional numbness, and fear, as well as experiencing frequent anxiety attacks or loss of appetite, and even a loss of immune function.[1]

Craig Eric Morris and Chris Reiber call this psychological phenomenon "Post-Relationship Grief." Which, for the purposes of simplicity, I will be referring to as "romantic grief." In a study of about 1700 people ages 18 to 52, Morris and Reiber found that 96 percent of respondents experienced some degree of emotional trauma during a breakup. A similar study from 2019 found evidence of depression in people who had recently suffered heartbreak—with many displaying a "lack of positive affect" in the days following the event. The authors concluded that, "[t]his is consistent with literature regarding grief."[2] Yet with all this research, romantic loss is not often culturally accepted as a form of grief.

By contrast, there are many structures in place—both clinical and social—to accommodate people who have experienced the death of someone close to them. I say "social" because I assume most of us are aware of the many etiquettes involved in supporting a bereaved person. We are expected to reach out frequently, engage in delicate language, and abide by a set of courtesies in order to cushion the blow of the loss. While not everyone will adhere to these norms, it is considered socially unacceptable to transgress them. But in the event of a breakup, the rules are far less rigid, and much less followed.

This is why the pain experienced during my breakup was understood as a form of "disenfranchised grief," which is defined as a "grief that persons experience when they incur a loss that is not or cannot be openly acknowledged, socially sanctioned or publicly mourned."[3] Traditional grief indeed has severe psychological implications, but the implications associated with disenfranchised grief have an added social element. This means that the person experiencing it may suffer alternative, interpersonal pains. It is important that we understand that "grief can arise in relation to any loss, and any loss can be the result of significant change, whether or not death is involved."[4]

In *The Year of Magical Thinking*, Joan Didion takes us through her grieving process in the twelve months following the sudden death of her husband, John Gregory Dunne. In remembering the loss of a man she loved for over four decades, Didion talks about warnings. She runs through ominous messages in her mind, and one in particular sticks out to her: John, a writer, predicted that he would never finish his book.

Belief as an omniscience on the part of the deceased is common among those who grieve them. The same happened in the weeks following my grandmother's death. My aunt told us that on Christmas Day, when she went to the hospital for the last time, my grandmother pulled her caretaker close to her. Rather than saying "Merry Christmas," as was expected, she whispered, "Send me flowers." This was a moment of great interest in my family. My grandmother had dementia, which makes this instance easy to dismiss as incoherent. But I believe it provided my aunt some spiritual comfort.

We get much clearer warnings with romantic failure. In the weeks leading up to my breakup, I could not wrap my head around the way the things had escalated. A month before, we had been in British Columbia, and I was meeting his extended family. We were laughing a lot and cooking meals with his parents. Did I know that, only a few weeks later, we would be crying in his apartment?

At what time did I want it to end? Was it at my birthday party *three weeks before*? Was it when I suggested we open up our relationship, *two weeks before*? When I got coffee with my friend and she recounted to me the days leading up to her own, very similar breakup, *a week before*? Or was it a year earlier, when we decided not to live together anymore? Didion had no real way to prepare for John's death, making her feelings of abandonment and helplessness all the more devastating: "I had no answers. I had no prognosis. I did not know how this had happened."[5] John's death was senseless. Our breakup was not. We are given so many warnings, and yet the loss still comes as a shock.

Didion, whose observational prose is clinical and sharp, was preoccupied with detail, often listing, ad nauseum, the names of people, places, and things she encounters in her life—as if to let us know that they did, in fact, exist. Her recounting of this difficult period is no different. In her grief, she engages in a Didion-esque sequence of behaviour—creating an inventory of all the places, dates, etc., leading up to John's death: "...read, learn, work it up, go to the literature. Information was control."[6] I call this a taxonomy of grief.

It's something I witnessed my mother do with regard to my grandmother. She would sit, staring fixedly at the floor, and trace the steps:

"It was 8pm when she fell in the hallway of your aunt's apartment on Christmas Day."

"She was wearing her favorite red sweater."

"We spent four hours together discussing the situation the night before she passed, and I had been in bed for three hours before they had gotten the call."

"At what time did this specific medical condition evolve into a worse one?"

In bereavement, we produce hard facts to make sense out of the senseless. This is not so different from a breakup. Memories of those final days are as clear as they are disorienting.

*Eternal Sunshine* strikes this balance very well. The film's timeline plays out in a reverse chronology. We begin with Joel's most recent memories and work our way backwards through time, where these earlier scenes take on a much more morose tone. In one scene, Joel and Clementine walk through a flea market. Clementine looks at families with children and says, wistfully, "I want to have a baby." After being pushed a couple more times, Joel responds, "Clementine, do you really think you could take care of a kid?" The scene escalates from there. Clementine, brash and quick-tempered, turns violently on Joel and the two begin to argue, inviting a crowd of onlookers.

The exacerbation of their innate differences, Clementine, gregarious and impulsive, Joel, meek and static, makes this fight too painful for Joel to revisit. As their surroundings begin to fade and people's faces become amorphous, he says, gratefully, "It's going." The film forgoes a lot of Kaufman's dialogue for the sake of pathos, allowing words to be absorbed into one another to emphasize Joel's panic. In this particular moment, we hear him mutter something along the lines of "oh the pain, the humiliation" which drowns into a bed of diegetic and non-diegetic sound. But in the script, Kaufman writes: "It's going, Clementine. All the crap and hurt and disappointment. It's all being wiped away."

This is one of many lines that Joel addresses Clementine in voiceover, speaking to her in hushed, intimate tones as he stumbles through his memories. Here, the anguish of having to remember such a dark period in their lives and the subsequent relief of its erasure, shows us how therapeutic the memory removal process may be.

The next memory is also morose. Joel and Clementine are eating dinner in a crowded Chinese restaurant. They are not speaking to one another. In Kaufman's script, Joel looks around and laments, in voiceover, "Is that like us? Are we just bored with each other? I can't stand the idea of being a couple that people think that about." This is changed in the film to "*You* can't stand the idea of being a couple that people think about." After taking a sip of her beer, which disgusts Joel, Clementine then initiates another fight—"Hey, would you do me a favor and clean the goddamn hair off the soap when you're done in the shower?" "Oh. Yeah. Okay," he responds. She presses on, "It's really gross. It's just, y'know, [Joel mouths the word, 'repulsive'] it's repulsive." Joel then hears the dialing of a phone, which is coming from Patrick back in the operating room. Joel looks beyond memory, where he sees Patrick standing in the restaurant window, which now looks into a bookstore. The scene transitions.

This moment taps into the very common idea that many long-term relationships devolve into mundanity. Over time, you grow so comfortable with one another that the relationship's edge begins to wane, and eventually the romantic spark is supplanted by an angry one. Joel and Clementine are sitting in total silence. And the *I* in "I can't stand the idea of being a couple that people think that about" becomes *you* to suggest that Clementine's following actions are a result of this fear. That the only solution to this hopelessly uninteresting moment is to start a fight.

My own relationship was plagued by a similar mundanity. We did not go on dates, we did not have sex, and we found that petty arguments were becoming commonplace. We were also fighting openly in front of our friends, something we vowed we would never do. And although there was a lot of crying in the early days of our breakup, even *that* starting feeling mundane. Flat line. Autopilot. He and I may have unconsciously known this. And so, like Clementine in the Chinese restaurant, we filled these gaps with anger, fighting publicly and going out of our way to make our breakup much more spectacular than our relationship had ever been.

Those final memories, as evidenced by these scenes in the film, are impossible to forget. They play out in your mind over and over again until it becomes too much. And then, with time, they become less potent. The pain begins to fade away, and all you can do is wait it out. But, thankfully, waiting is not the only option in *Eternal Sunshine*.

Grief associated with death is defined by its finality. You have to grapple with the idea that someone can never be in your life again. When it comes to romantic grief, however, the door is always open, especially if there is geographical or social contact. In the case of my breakup, we lived close by and operated within the same nebulous friend group. My grief was an ever-opening wound, making it up to me, the bereaved, to create distance. But this is no easy feat. It's why people find excuses to call each other, or insist to their friends that they are indeed capable of being in the same room together. It's why people continue to sleep together months after the relationship has ended. Even if your exchanges are sparse and clipped, corporate tones are simply not enough. Because, as Charles Dickens writes in *Nicholas Nickleby*, "Love, however, is very materially assisted by a warm and active imagination: which has a long memory, and will thrive, for a considerable time, on very slight and sparing food."[7]

Many reach the conclusion, somewhere along the timeline, that more drastic measures are needed. *Eternal Sunshine* capitulates to this idea, which is why it occupies such a special place in the genre of romance movies. The premise for the film came by way of Gondry's friend Pierre Bismuth. Bismuth, a prolific artist, had played around with the concept of sending a card to people stating that they had been erased from the memory of a former lover. This was conceived originally as an art project, but Bismuth allowed Gondry to run with the idea instead. In his reasoning Gondry says that, "because I have trouble in romance, this idea appealed to me enormously."[8] And so, he set out to make a film about the (un)finality of romantic grief and all its attendant miseries.

There is a psychological core to romantic grief which stems from the fact that people are unable to forget each other. "I've always been interested in how memories can make us feel good or really hurt us," says Gondry, "even though they don't really exist."[9] He and Bismuth discovered that there was truth in the idea that, given the opportunity, a person really would opt to be rid of their painful memories, even if that means forgetting about someone important to them. Memories can be torture. In breakups especially, we obsess over them, lying awake at night inching through every cumulative infraction. Understanding romantic loss as a form of grief comes with an acceptance that this experience can be traumatic and painful. Cataloging details, obsessing over warnings, and parsing through fraught memories make the process of a breakup an infernal burden on the mind. If I had the opportunity to forget him, would I take it?

Late in the game, Kaufman decided to name the film "Eternal Sunshine of the Spotless Mind," a line from Alexander's Pope's

1717 poem, "Eloisa to Abelard." The poem is derived from the tragic medieval love story between a young pupil, Héloïse d'Argenteuil' (changed later to Eloisa), and her much older teacher, Peter Abelard. Legend has it that upon finding out about Eloisa and Abelard's affair, her family kidnaps Abelard and castrates him—leading Abelard to join a monastery, and Eloisa a covenant. The poem, a heroic epistle, plays out an exchange between the two lovers years after being ripped apart. Eloisa expresses the torment of her unrequited love, and the overwhelming desire to forget him:

> How happy is the blameless vestal's lot!
> The world forgetting, by the world forgot.
> Eternal sunshine of the spotless mind!
> Each pray'r accepted, and each wish resign'd;
> Labour and rest, that equal periods keep;
> "Obedient slumbers that can wake and weep;"
> Desires compos'd, affections ever ev'n,
> Tears that delight, and sighs that waft to Heav'n.
> Grace shines around her with serenest beams,
> And whisp'ring angels prompt her golden dreams.
> For her th' unfading rose of Eden blooms,
> And wings of seraphs shed divine perfumes,

For her the Spouse prepares the bridal ring,
For her white virgins hymeneals sing,
To sounds of heav'nly harps she dies away,
And melts in visions of eternal day.

The first four lines of the stanza are delivered in the film by Mary to Dr. Mierzwiak in a bid to impress him. Mary, characterized rather harshly by A.O Scott as "a semi-clueless autodidact" in his 2004 review of the film, unconsciously invokes Eloisa's words to express to Mierzwiak that the suffering of unrequited love is too great.[10] The spotless woman Eloisa illustrates, and who Mary alludes to, is one who lives in a state of grace: "Grace shines around her with serenest beams." She has peaceful sleeps, "[a]nd whisp'ring angels prompt her golden dreams." And she dies happily, "[t]o sounds of heav'nly harps she dies away," and free of sin, "[f]or her th' unfading rose of Eden blooms." How blissful it would be, say Mary and Eloisa, to just forget.

It has been over a year since my breakup and, still, I am crying into my pillow at night. I go through long periods of numbness, but the gloom hangs overhead. I harbor resentment towards friends who opt to spend more time with him than me. I feel suffocated by the city I grew up in, one that he is foreign to. I drink heavily at parties, watching him place his new girlfriend on his lap. In these moments, the numbness fades and in its place comes sorrow, sometimes rage. The disenfranchisement of my grief is such that I can no longer tell anecdotes about him in casual conversation. The grace period for anger has run up and I can no longer rant about him to my friends or parents. My friends are choosing to spend time with him and to foster their own separate friendships. They are inviting him and his new girlfriend to cottages and showing up to parties together. The window of grief, if there ever was one, has closed and I am expected to move on, to have found someone else or to be comfortable enough with myself to just not care. My anger and sadness no longer have a place. They have to go.

When my grandmother died, I called him to tell him of her passing. We cried into the phone and the moment was sweet. I half-heartedly invited him to the funeral but when the day came, I hoped to see him. When it was over, I scanned the crowd and felt a surge of disappointment. He had not come. But was it disappointment? I had just said goodbye to my grandmother for the last time and, simultaneously, I was also saying goodbye to him. There was no real obligation for him to show up to the funeral. Most likely, he felt like he was overstepping. And that was something I had to accept.

That day, I experienced a fleeting feeling that, like Joel and Clementine, we would find our way back to each other. If not romantically—I was not ready for that—then spiritually. Like Joel and Clementine, there could be something pulling us together and the many, many times we had caused each other harm in the past year did not matter.

I am now moving to New York, in part because I want to embrace new experiences. Also, because I need a fresh start, away from the memories, regrets, and the suffocating, all-consuming agony of my romantic grief. The pain of realizing this may not be us, that the aspirational way with which I viewed Joel and Clementine in the early days of our romance was false, is too much to handle. Perhaps, if it was possible, a spotless mind would be the best answer.

## Two: Writing the Spotless Mind

When reflecting on his then two decade-long career to David Ehrlich of *IndieWire* in 2016, Charlie Kaufman said, "I feel like I fucking blew it." At the time, Kaufman was stewing in his disappointment over the commercial failures of *Synecdoche, New York* and *Anomalisa*, his first two attempts in the director's seat. Now, anyone who has seen these films would say to Kaufman that his work is a treasure, and that he shouldn't feel so defeated. Ehrlich himself is clearly frustrated with Kaufman's attitude, but acknowledges rather sagely that, "[a]s you sit there and listen to him self-diagnose, it occurs to you that he interrogates himself better than you ever could."[11]

Of course, disappointment is normal for any artist who feels their work has failed in one sense or another. But for Kaufman, it's a way of being. He insists that his public face is "a little less morose" than the one he wears in private. Yet even in interviews, his pessimism is palpable. Responding to Ehrlich's futile attempt to cheer him up, he says, "[h]ope springs eternal. But I tend towards depression."[12]

Chronic disappointment is often accompanied by self-doubt, which is a feeling Kaufman knows well. His childhood aspirations for the stage exemplify this. As a child, he was obsessed with the theater, spending precious hours reading Guare, Wilson, Beckett, and Ionesco. He was also an active member of his high school drama club, and even played the lead in a school production of *Play it Again, Sam* despite his timid demeanor. It seemed inevitable, then, that when it came time for college, Kaufman would pursue this passion full-time at acting school. But by the end of his first year, he had switched majors: "I think I became self-conscious. I was very shy, and I became kind of embarrassed about it."[13]

Doubt is a consumptive thing. But throughout history, and especially since the Enlightenment, it has become a pillar of wisdom. Greatness comes with the acceptance of uncertainty and, for esteemed critic Robert Hughes, this is especially true for artists. Writing about a Cezanne exhibition in 1996, Hughes looks to the anxiety-laden artist's final painting to excavate some inner truth about the artist's talent. For Hughes, while the painting is much more structured than Cezanne's larger body of work, its misshapen figures barely conceal the reality of the artist's inner tumult. The painting stands at the precipice of madness, only just holding it together. Hughes summarizes Cezanne's legacy as such: "The greater the artist, the greater the doubt. Perfect confidence is granted to the less talented as a consolation prize."[14]

Self-sabotaging, pessimistic, and timid as he is, Kaufman is not oblivious to his shortcomings. Like Cezanne, his career is actually *propelled* by shortcomings. Kaufman's protagonists are anxious, fractured, and self-effacing—moving about their worlds in a state of sheer, exhaustive panic. *Adaptation*, the 2002 meta-comedy, which Kaufman wrote about his struggle to adapt *The Orchid Thief*, has Nicholas Cage playing two leads: the fictional Charlie Kaufman, a spiritually impotent, neurotic writer; and Kaufman's fictional twin (credited in the film as a co-writer), an uninhibited sweetheart. In the film, the Charlie character's greatest obstacle is self-doubt. In two separate scenes, he dithers in voiceover about whether or not he should follow through with a simple action (consummating a romantic date and speaking to Susan Orlean in an elevator). On both occasions, he is unable to act on his desires. Especially when paired against his twin, who is a less talented writer but more capable of realizing his work, it's obvious that Charlie is stunted by fear. Charlie is a proxy for Kaufman himself, but more interestingly, he is a proxy for how Kaufman *perceives* himself. Interviewers have noted Kaufman's ease and candor when they meet him face-to-face, yet Cage's Charlie is incapable of the most basic social gestures. Charlie is exaggerated in his timidity to the extent that it is only when his brother tragically dies and his book subject is eaten by a crocodile (fictitiously) that he is finally able to feel unencumbered in his writing.

Doubt is the rupture of belief. Self-doubt, therefore, is the rupture of belief in who we are, and what we are capable of. It requires stepping outside the self and warning it not to go any further—each step forward is unknown and terrifying. *Being John Malkovich*, Kaufman's most commercially successful film after *Eternal Sunshine*, opens on a marionette puppet sitting alone in his bedroom. The puppet walks up to his little mirror and looks at his own reflection. Eyes widening, he backs away in terror, smashing objects as he hurls about the room. He smashes the mirror, shattering it, and then looks up at the person operating his strings—Craig, a puppeteer and the greasy protagonist of the movie. The puppet begins to dance, twirling and flying across the stage. His dancing grows more erratic until he eventually collapses on the floor in exasperation. We later learn that Craig has named this sequence "The Dance of Disillusionment."

If we are to acknowledge this wider theme of self-doubt, the chain of command would go puppet's strings pulled by

*Eternal Sunshine: Auteur*

Craig, Craig's strings pulled by Kaufman. He is an artist who watches and obsesses over his most fascinating subject: the self (or rather, *himself*.) Even in periods where he is not working, this remains to be true: "I've [...] seen critics say 'This is a Charlie Kaufman-type movie, and so-and-so made it.' And it's like... why do *they* get to make Charlie Kaufman movies and I don't? I think about that all the time."[15] Because, in the Charlie Kaufman universe, life is a reel of memories that renders us useless in its passage.

In a 2020 article for the *New Yorker* titled "Can Charlie Kaufman Get Out of His Head?" Jon Baskin locates two very similar sequences in *Being John Malkovich* and *Eternal Sunshine*, where the characters dart in and out of fading sceneries. In the former, it's Lotte (Craig's girlfriend) and Maxine (Lotte and Craig's love interest) running through John Malkovich's memories to escape Craig. In the latter. it's Joel and Clementine running through Joel's deteriorating memories. In both instances, the characters find themselves inside of someone's head, bearing witness to the mind's most shameful memories—Joel caught in the act of self-gratification, Malkovich watching his parents have sex. Baskin finds that these scenes say a lot about Kaufman's worldview, where his characters must grapple with "a band of unease about the porousness of self and other, past and present, real and imaginary."[16]

Often, the characters are consumed by self-loathing. Craig is unsatisfied with the life he's built with Lotte, reeling at the failure of his puppeteering career and unable to come to terms with the fact that Maxine doesn't want him. In *Eternal Sunshine*, Joel and Clementine hate who they've become in their relationship. Here, Kaufman investigates the idea that, often, in romantic relationships, we become the worst versions of ourselves. For example, near the end of the film, Joel and Clementine find the tapes that Mary has left for them. Apprehensively, they play them aloud and are mortified by what they hear. The tapes are recordings of Joel and Clementine listing everything they hate about one another during the intake process for the procedure. Joel paints Clementine as simple-minded, slutty, and insecure. Clementine characterizes Joel as meek and pathetic. She then says something that sends Joel over the edge, leading him to kick her out of his car: "He's boring. I've been thinking how I was before and how I am now and it's like he changed me. I feel like I'm always pissy. I don't like myself when I'm with him. I don't like myself anymore."

As their relationship begins to age, Joel and Clementine embody these negative qualities. Being with Clementine, Joel settles into his role as a passive, judgemental sad boy. And in that gap, Clementine becomes bigger, louder, more abrasive and more drunk. In many ways they are the antithesis of one another, yet they are also mirrors for their own worst traits. And like Craig's puppet, they don't like what they see. When Joel and Clementine look at one another, they are no longer able to recognize *themselves*. In this way, Kaufman reclaims his self-doubt by using it as a guiding principle in his art.

After speaking to Kaufman, Ehrlich wonders if he uses art as a tool for control—"control of a production, control of a body, control of space and time and memory." And jumping down the chain of command from Kaufman to Craig, one has to ask what his characters do to cope with their self-doubt. Control also plays an important role here. In the same way Kaufman creates doubles of himself, his characters sever themselves from their own agonizing interior lives. They ask, does separating the mind from the body afford us control? When Craig finds a portal into John Malkovich's head which allows him to live the life of a successful person, he refuses to leave. Malkovich's mind is feeble enough for Craig to seize control of the portal, leaving room for him to tailor Malkovich's life to the one he has dreamed for himself. Similarly, Joel and Clementine, rather than facing themselves and the people they have become in their relationship, decide to take control and have it zapped from memory.

But there are no easy fixes in a Kaufman film and, ultimately, Joel and Clementine's attempts at control are futile. By Kaufman's design, the decisions these characters make leave them worse off than they were before. At the end of *Being John Malkovich*, Craig becomes trapped inside the portal, forced to watch Lotte and Maxine spend the rest of their lives together, blissfully in love. His dogged lust for Maxine and his own self-hatred condemn him to an eternity of longing. In *Eternal Sunshine*, Joel and Clementine find their way back to each other in the end. As Baskin puts it, "what is really accursed about consciousness is that the strip cannot be snipped."[17] Or, in other words, one can never escape the agony of their own existence.

Like Joel and Clementine, Kaufman realized when writing *Eternal Sunshine* that maybe things are not as simple as they seem. He has always been firm that writing does not come easy to him. His process takes a great deal of planning, combing, and revising. And while *The Orchid Thief* was tough, *Eternal Sunshine* was Everest waiting for him on the other side of the mountain. The story, which is intricately layered and winding, was a difficult one to map out. Kaufman's major hurdle was conceiving of ways to visualize a fading memory while maintaining a cohesive narrative. Joel needed to exist inside of his memories, while at the same time reacting and responding to them, while at the same time interacting with Clementine as her past and present self. Memory-Clementine cannot respond to Joel because the memory has already played out, but there needed to be a way for Joel to speak to her as his present self. Make sense? Probably not.

Kaufman and Gondry came to a compromise and decided that Joel should be able to react to his surroundings in carefully-placed voiceover narration—being able to comment on his memories and demonstrate an awareness of his surroundings. This way, he could speak to Clementine in his mind without his characters saying them aloud in the memory and disrupting the flow of the scene.

The film also plays out in such a way that Joel's memories are being incrementally erased. So, if Joel is, in one scene, in a bookstore with Clementine and, in the next, on a beach in Montauk, he cannot technically remember the bookstore. But it's particularly tricky to write a character arc where the character learns and grows without being able to remember a majority of scenes in the film. So again, Kaufman worked with Gondry to make it so that the memories would degrade—books losing their color, houses falling to pieces, faces transforming into blobs. This clever use of visual effects shows the viewer that Joel's memories are fading, but not so much as to disappear completely. In the final version he can jump into a scene with a faint understanding of what has just transpired, and the plot can move forward coherently. The great challenge of screenwriting, in Kaufman's mind, is that film is a static artform:

> What I find interesting is trying to create a script that makes you need to go back and look at it again; and that the second time you look at it, you'll see things that you didn't see, that you couldn't have seen the first time because you didn't have the information that you have by the end of the first viewing. So, the second viewing becomes the viewing of a different movie, even though it's exactly the same movie.[18]

He echoes this idea often and locates that the only thing which changes about a film is the audience's relation to it. Therefore, what he offers with his scripts is a sense of uncertainty, because you can watch a movie five years later, "and have a different experience because you're a different

*Eternal Sunshine: Auteur*

person."[19] He achieves this effect by crafting his films as a sort of hologram, one which looks different depending on where you stand. In a way, he likes to destabilize everything you see in the film. For example, an interviewer once deigned to pin *Being John Malkovich* down to a theme, suggesting that Lotte's chimp Elijah is "the only heroic character" in the movie.[20] To this, Kaufman was infuriatingly ambiguous: "Is Elijah heroic? He seems to be rather heroic, but who really knows what's going on inside him."

It's frustrating, but this "up in the air" quality breathes new life into Kaufman's work upon repeat viewings. And although his plots are complicated, increasingly so over the years, there is an element to Kaufman's work that does feel fixed. Narrative complexity is only a scaffolding for what really matters, at least for me, to Kaufman's most successful works: emotional groundedness.

*Eternal Sunshine* contains elements of sci-fi—its premise relies on a memory-removal technology that has yet to be invented. But sci-fi is a second thought for Kaufman. As he told *Vulture* in 2015, "I wanted to do something about relationships, and when I was writing it, I'd feel like I was having to pay too much attention to the science-fiction element of it. I didn't want that to get in the way of the exploration of what a relationship actually looks like in people's heads."[21] There is a devastating realism to the way Joel and Clementine's relationship dissolves. There is no cheating. No grand heartbreak. Only two people imploding together.

And as much as Joel and Clementine can no longer recognize themselves, they also fail to recognize each other at every juncture of the relationship. As David La Rocca puts it in his philosophical inquiry of Kaufman's works, "[e]xistential and continental philosophers have been known to dwell on the way the other feels irreproachably distant from oneself—on the other side of a liminal space that can never be crossed. As a result, we are and remain unknown to each other."[22] There is something opaque to all of us, and the dissolution of romantic relationships makes this all too clear. No matter how much time you spend with another person, no matter how intimate you become, no matter if you think you know every facet of their mind (maybe better than they do), you can never really penetrate their *soul*. He might have achieved the great feat of colonizing John Malkovich's mind, but Craig has no interest in really *being* Malkovich— abusing his consent and overriding his decisions every step of the way. *Being John Malkovich* proselytizes that people are far too wrapped up in their own inner turmoil to really see beyond themselves. This is especially true in relationships. The great tragedy of breakups is that the person we spent so much time with is often an illusory figure we have conjured from our own minds. A person we *wish* to be dating.

Breakups are defined by doubt. Did I make the right choice? Was it all for nothing? Who was I in this relationship? Did I like who I was?

In the months following my breakup, I was hit with an unwanted clarity about the person I had spent the last five years of my life with—a clarity which shook everything I had previously believed about us. Moments from two, four years back were being pieced together in my mind, forming an entirely new person than the one I had loved—one who was hurting more than I allowed myself to believe. Much more afraid than I had ever caught onto. A person living with an impregnable inner life that made him unknowable to me. I told him this during one of our many endless phone calls, "I don't know who you are." His voice cracked, "It really hurts to hear you say that." But I really didn't know—he was a complicated person who I had only glossed the surface of, more troubled than I had ever realized. Endlessly capable of deceit. This was perhaps the greatest heartbreak of it all, that all these strides I had made in learning to love, care for, and truly see another person may not have really happened at all.

LaRocca describes Kaufman as an "emotional realist" in the sense that he is not so much concerned with representing life as it is, but life as we *feel* it.[23] His skill is born of the way he digs to the emotional core of his characters. We do not know Joel. He is not especially expressive. He is often quiet, a wallflower to his environment. Joel's journey is (literally) impossible for us to experience. But we understand how he feels—that he is angry at Clementine, that he is scared and alone, that he is indescribably sad. Kaufman doesn't get too bogged down in the logic of his worlds, but rather, as LaRocca writes, "He uses fabrication and fabulation—a playful use of 'lies' and the 'fake'—to achieve emotional realism."[24] The emotional truth of *Eternal Sunshine* is dialectical—romantic relationships are at once both real and fake. The things I believed about my relationship, or the things Joel and Clementine believed about each other, did not exist. But our feelings about them did.

This is where I arrive at an impasse. If Kaufman's narratives are unstable, but the emotions are fixed, how could it be then that I experienced such monumentally different emotions watching *Eternal Sunshine* on either end of my relationship?

Well, in his reticence, Kaufman waited until the very end of the film to destabilize our feelings about it. Joel and Clementine stand face-to-face in Joel's hallway. Clementine repeats her tagline, "I'm just a fucked-up girl looking for my own peace of mind." Joel raises his arms in defeat: "I can't see anything that I don't like about you." "But you will!" replies Clementine. "You will think of things. And I'll get bored with you and feel trapped because that's what happens with me." "Okay" he shrugs, smiling. "Okay" she breathes. Clementine begins to cry and the two of them laugh, nervous but hopeful. The final scene has Joel and Clementine running together up the snowy beach in Montauk as Beck's "Everybody's Gotta Learn Sometime" plays for a second time.

Kaufman's texts are not prescriptive: "I've never and I will never talk about what anything I write is about."[25] Which gave way to the moment where, after finishing the film on the day of my breakup, I sat up straight and said in a flurry of tears, "Wait. Why am I sad?" When I watched it five years before, I had always turned off *Eternal Sunshine* happy that Joel and Clementine had reconciled. I found beauty and comfort that they were on a teleological path which led them back to one another. Now I found it grotesque. The movie gave me no answer about their futures. The sickening knowledge that they would, someday, inevitably settle back into their worst selves, become deluded and hateful as they were before, seemed now invariably depressing. Out of a five-year relationship, the film left me with an entirely different feeling.

It was the hologram. And looking at it from this end I was, once again, filled with doubt.

## Three: Michel's Grief

It's 2003, and Michel Gondry is at a Virgin Megastore in Hollywood, sitting for a Q&A with fellow music video directors, Chris Cunningham and Spike Jonze.[26] The three are seated at a long table with a large audience before them, who wait patiently for a turn at the mic. The moderator hops around the room, his foot dragging nakedly behind him, in a struggle to attend to every raised hand. Few of the questions are directed at Gondry.

"Could you guys tell us some anecdotes about how you came up with the idea for a particular video?" asks one guy.

"Maybe, like, Spike how you came up with the idea for the dog dying in the Daft Punk video?"

"Or Chris, how you came up with the idea for the Bjork robot video? And Michel… you know… pick something."

The audience laughs. Gondry looks irritated. In a heavy French accent, he interjects, "Can we have a moderator with two shoes?" One of the event coordinators responds, "Ty sprained his ankle skating on the way here, but he's still giving

45

it his all!" Everyone claps. Gondry does not.

As the session proceeds, Gondry plays with his fingers and chuckles sparingly. A girl asks Cunningham, "What's the most recent song you've heard that you wanted to make a video for?" Cunningham replies, "'Rock Your Body'" by Justin Timberlake. Everyone laughs, and the girl presses, "I want a real answer." "I'm serious!" insists Cunningham. The moderator tries to move along, but Gondry leans towards Cunningham and says "You cannot answer properly. You did not answer her." Cunningham looks miffed. "Don't you think the Justin Timberlake track is a good track?" "No, I prefer to listen to Michael Jackson, it's the same but even better," says Gondry. "He's the new Michael Jackson" declares Cunningham. "It's not the new Michael Jackson," replies Gondry, imperious, "it doesn't bring anything." A smattering of nervous laughter follows. Cunningham shrugs, visibly annoyed. Gondry then provides his own answer to the question (which was never asked of him): "But I'd like to do a video for Mya." He looks down sheepishly. "She's really pretty."

In this minute-long exchange, Gondry presents himself as a deeply frustrating person. He is abrasive and self-righteous, unafraid to sharpen the air with hostility. But there is something endearing about him. By the end of this terse back-and-forth, everyone is shaking their heads at him and smiling, a response most often provoked by curmudgeonly old men and petulant little boys.

This conflicting sensibility is indelible to Gondry's work. Developing his childhood interest in photography into a vocation for film, he has always used art to soften the prickly realities of daily life. His works are highly imaginative. Yet, shining through as it does in the Q&A, is a compulsive honesty. He pinpoints that tricky intersection of "macabre" and "childlike" which makes up the ethereal. So much so that the long-standing collaboration between he and Bjork, the queen of ethereality herself, seems almost fated:

> But it is true that creativity is very much associated with a certain form of immaturity" he says. "When you become an adult you often have to limit your creativity—I mean, you can still be creative if you are working in a system—but if you do creativity that is only connected to pleasure, then you make big electric trains and you seem to be either a child molester or a big kid. I am a little bit of a big kid. It's a subject I talk about with Björk a lot. Sometimes she says, "I think it's time you should move on to something

more adult," and I think she's right because she is very smart and she's generally right. But if being [sic] adult is becoming cynical or pretentious then I prefer to stay immature.[27]

This unwavering commitment to immaturity has paid off for Gondry. Having risen to international attention through their creative partnership, he echoes Bjork's bizarre and wondrous music with his own whimsy. He brought acclaim to the music video genre through an extensive repertoire of videos for other artists as well, such as Sinead O'Connor, Lucas Secon, Daft Punk, The White Stripes, The Chemical Brothers, The Vines, Steriogram, Radiohead, and Beck. The Youtube comment sections for many of the popular songs he's worked on are often littered with remarks about the mastery of their videos. It's no surprise, then, that Gondry has won a number of awards for direction.

Gondry's videos are often impressionistic, with their high contrast lighting and rich, saturated palettes. He plays with size, placing his human subjects in oversized sets and maneuvering them through deconstructed, moving stages. Gondry is intent on creating things by hand, allowing human error to shine proudly through his work: "The idea that it's made by hand makes it unique. It's not coming from a factory or a machine so it cannot be reproduced. It's like something very strict but created in chaos. I think there is an honesty to have in what you do."[28] His aptitude for transitions, together with these practical effects, requires a great degree of choreography. These transitions, a camera turning on its head into a dollhouse which then becomes a chair, for example, beg the viewer to peer into Gondry's secret worlds. These worlds are eclectic and rickety. His camera careens through starry nightscapes and topsy-turvy bedrooms. Yet despite how artificial they look, the videos are oddly affecting—cut, always, with a mournful edge. As Lynn Hirschberg observes in the *New York Times*, "Most of Gondry's ideas seem to spring out of romantic turmoil or joy (or both)."[29] It's that emotional immediacy in his work which gives it such vitality.

In a 2004 interview with Gondry, Charlie Rose makes a rather astute observation. "There is something about you that reminds me of Charlie Kaufman. I don't know what it is… maybe it's youth. You guys seem so young."

Much like his creative union with Bjork, a collaboration with weirdo-genius, Charlie Kaufman, was inevitable. Fresh off the success of *Being John Malkovich*, Kaufman came on to write Gondry's feature debut, *Human Nature*. The film, which stars Patricia Arquette, Tim Robbins, and Rhys Ifans, is about an unusually hairy naturalist, an "ape" man, and a poorly-endowed scientist, whose "otherness" cannot contain what is inescapable for each one of them... human nature. While the film is characteristic of both Gondry and Kaufman's larger bodies of work—focusing on themes of repression, identity, and lust—it is woefully devoid of whimsy. Gondry's kinetic camerawork and stylized set pieces are missing here, as is Kaufman's wit and unusual penchant for empathy. The visuals are flat, and there is a knowingness to the performances which makes you feel sleazy for watching. Although the characters are placed on a tragic path, the film dissuades the viewer from empathizing with them. As Arquette pornographically breathes through her lines, and Ifhans cartoonishly humps his surroundings, their plight rings hollow. As Nathan Rabin writes for the *A. V. Club*, "That is perhaps the tragedy of *Human Nature*: Despite its title and abundance of brilliant ideas and clever lines, it feels strangely abstract and theoretical."[30]

Audiences and critics of the time caught onto this sense of abstraction, and the film was a critical and commercial flop. *Human Nature* is about the unbearable agony of living, but ultimately this message is informed too heavily by the curmudgeon in Gondry and Kaufman, and not enough by the child. They admit it themselves. "I think we share a common negativity" said Gondry. "Once, I was talking to Björk, and she said to me, 'You're the most pessimistic person, but at least you're funny.' And I think that's something you could say about Charlie, as well."[31] It's a marvel they made another film together.

Gondry's best work contains a strong element of vitality, in the same way Rabin finds Kaufman's best work to feel "gloriously, painfully alive." Whatever vitality that's lacking in *Human Nature*, however, Gondry spills enthusiastically into *Eternal Sunshine*. When Gondry moved to the United States, he understood one word out of ten, and thus, when presented with a song for his next music video, he would "recreate whatever was said based on those few words."[32] The entire concept of the film, "what if you could erase painful memories?" comes out of this simple notion. There is something very childish to the idea: if I don't like something, why can't I just make it go away? Yet, like the untarnished psychology of a child, it is unexpectedly wise. *Eternal Sunshine* encompasses that duality so integral to Gondry's being. On the one hand, jaded, and on the other, precocious.

But wisdom cannot save us from our base emotions. An

event that occurred during the making of *Eternal Sunshine* pushed Gondry to settle into the more pessimistic side of himself. When asked whether making movies is therapeutic for him, Gondry said "no." "Making them you get left by your girlfriend and you have only bad memories attached to it," he explained. "You don't sleep, you take sleeping pills, you gain weight. It is definitely not healthy or therapeutic."[33]

Michel Gondry's early days in New York were bittersweet. He had moved there from France with his girlfriend, BK, to shoot *Eternal Sunshine*, shortly after his father had passed away. For Gondry, those days were marked by loss but also hope: "While I was finding various ways to see Joel Barrish's memories of Clementine evaporate, fade, decay, I was building my own with BK."[34]

Gondry and BK spent a year in New York together. She decorated his apartment with her eclectic sensibilities and the two carved out a life for themselves, forging moments that would later become too painful for Gondry to recall: "Like this time we went to visit Ellen, the Director of Photography, in the snowy upstate, or when we had this dinner in this sushi place and BK overheard this customer commenting on my accoutrement 'this guy sure is ready for a storm.' She couldn't stop laughing for a while after that."[35] In Gondry's mind, both the movie and his relationship with BK were running along smoothly, but this sentiment was held by him alone. As the film entered its editing stages, BK told Gondry she wanted out. She was moving to Los Angeles.

The breakup was devastating for Gondry. "I am ashamed to say that the pain was greater than the one I had felt for my father," he remembers. "Sometimes I was crying so hard in the street I had to stop walking because I couldn't see the pavement anymore."[36] Here, Gondry is poking at the rather taboo idea that the pain of a breakup can sometimes feel more acute than the pain of losing a loved one.

I lost my grandmother on January 3, 2023. Her death, while anticipated for years as her health deteriorated steadily, nevertheless sent shockwaves through my family. Three weeks after that I was abruptly dumped by someone I had only been dating for a month, and, like Gondry, I am ashamed to say that that pain felt more acute. Of course, my reaction was likely compounded by the death of my grandmother. But when she died, I only cried. When I was dumped, I threw things. I punched the floor. I told my roommate I didn't know if I could make it through the night. I think that the shock of the dumping had superseded the dull, blunted pain of losing a woman who I had known and loved my entire life. Grieving my grandmother took preparation; grieving a one-month relationship meant shoveling dirt into an empty grave of unfulfilled experiences. But my grandmother will linger in my head every day for the rest of my life, whereas I recovered from being dumped within a month. Looking back, the pain of losing my five-year relationship is more akin to losing my grandmother, blunt and ongoing—but unlike her death, I expect it will be less impactful over time.

After he and BK split up, Gondry ran through a series of futile questions: "Did I neglect her? I don't know. I think I grew older. I mean physically. BK became more pretty while I grew uglier, or something really pathetic. I was pathetic. I am pathetic."[37] After my own relationship ended, we circled these same questions. On Boxing Day, we walked around the city, stopping frequently to sit and cry. Sometimes we cried while we were walking, unabashed at confused strangers passing by. That day, he recounted what hindsight had told him—that he never tried to properly understand me. That he took me for granted. That he thought I needed him when, in fact, it was really he who needed me. These were all things I already knew. I was providing a soft, invisible support that kept him running for five years. This is not to say he did not return that support,

*Eternal Sunshine: Auteur*

but that he never felt my half of the weight until it was gone. His acute emotional suffering occurred right at the moment I rubbed his back and said we should no longer be together. Mine began about six months before that.

Gondry harbors a profound attachment to physical objects. After his breakup with BK, he kept a box full of knick knacks that he made after she left him. A necklace made out of his own fingernails. A Nike sneaker with a doll shoved in it, its tiny plastic hand holding a key to their shared apartment. BK's name scraped together with pages from a book. A misshapen bra. "I made this because her breasts were two different sizes."[38] It's no secret that Gondry is an oddball. A cursory look at his body of work should tell you as much. So it seems almost natural that he should contain his pain within oddities and trinkets.

On the day of my own breakup, I was on my way out the door, blinded by my own tears, when he yelled "wait!" and disappeared back into the living room. He came back holding a photobooth strip we had taken a couple years back—our faces smushed together and beaming. In one of the photos our mouths were wide open, frozen in laughter. Silently, he pulled a pair of scissors out of a drawer and cut the strip in half. He held one of the halves out in his hand and said, "please take it." The strip was magnetized to my fridge for the better part of a year, until it became unbecoming to display. It's now sitting in my nightstand. I have other memorabilia of this sort lying around my room, less naked to the untrained eye. A Clipper lighter we bought together in Paris, blue with a blue cocktail on it; a bar of Castabel soap that his mother gave me; a quarter-zip sweater he had worn in every photo from his vacation to San Francisco; a little toy car we bought on a trip to his favorite board game store; a custom-made *Eternal Sunshine* T-shirt he gave me one year for my birthday.

Gondry's box of oddities may seem unusual, but to anyone who has experienced romantic grief, his behavior is uncomfortably familiar. The idiosyncrasies that make up our intimate knowledge of another person, or a shared moment between the two partners, are fundamental memories that are integral to the romantic grieving process. In Eternal Sunshine, Ellen Kuras's camera fixates on the extreme detail of certain objects. Especially in Joel's memories, the camera hyper-focuses on the threads of a quilt, a black-and-white photograph, the eye of a babydoll. As the objects come into focus, it becomes clear that they remind him of Clementine. The *mise-en-scène* is extra detailed because the more there is for Joel to miss, the more there is to lose—or in the context of the film, the more that will disappear. Gondry explains in interviews that Lacuna Inc. is a device to explore nostalgia, a feeling he describes as "uncontrollable": "I was reading in a book about the brain that we have the feeling of nostalgia when we think of a memory because the mind knows it is a moment of time that will never appear again."[39] When Patrick is rummaging through the stolen items that Clementine submitted before undergoing her memory removal procedure, it is clear that they are alien to him. His attempts to reignite a passion in Clementine by harvesting information from them fall short because he was not a part of the memories they are attached to.

While they may be random inanimate trinkets, a shell necklace or a photograph taped to crumpled lined paper, they have nostalgic value. Their magic lies in the fact that they belong to moments which only Joel and Clementine experienced. Memories they can never experience again. When we grieve a relationship, we grieve those lost, happy times. These are times that we could not recreate as our relationships decay, and they are certainly not times we can create when we are estranged. So, we desperately cling to physical memorabilia that will trigger these lost times and allow us to relive them, even just for a moment.

Gondry created his box of oddities as his own form of

post-breakup therapy. But there was another box as well, one that he would not keep: "She had left abruptly, saying she had to think and would make her decision in the weeks to come. I knew too well the outcome and the anxiety was eating me from inside, so I went to Office Depot, bought the biggest cardboard box, and packed all BK's clothes and mementoes."[40]

In the film, Joel is seen rummaging through his house after deciding to go through with the procedure. He combs through anything that may have an attachment to Clementine and puts them in a bag. Gondry recalls that, after BK left, this was not a "film moment" for him anymore. It was real. And now he could no longer watch *Eternal Sunshine*.

## Four: Forgetting

In one scene in *Eternal Sunshine*, Mary rants to Stan about the benefits of their work. "You look at a baby and it's so pure and so clean, adults are this mess of phobias," she waxes, "and Howard just makes it all go away."

What she's getting at here is that adults, through their years of lived experience, grow embittered to the world around them. They carry a heavy load of painful and confusing memories which renders them, as Mary says, a "mess of phobias." As a character, Mary poses a crucial juxtaposition to Joel and Clementine because, unlike the leading couple, she is stuck in a situation where, working under Howard's employ, she is forced to relive these painful memories every day. Howard tells Joel in their consultation that, "[there's an emotional core to our memories, and when you eradicate that core then the degradation happens." It's not the detail itself, color, sound, or smell, which hurts us, but the feeling associated with it. So if Joel and Clementine remained estranged from one another, these feelings would begin to fade, whereas Mary's, with the constant presence of Howard, would not.

The memory-removal element of the film may be fictitious, but in a sense we all have our own procedures for forgetting, whether that's by moving cities or countries, ripping up old pictures, or getting rid of nostalgic belongings. Ultimately, Eternal Sunshine came out at a time when, if you wanted to never see someone again, your chances of succeeding were high. But twenty-years out, and about ten from the advent of social media, we're living in an era where we are all Marys. The entire project of social media is to collapse time and space, and "connect" people through the sharing of text, images, and videos at a pace and convenience the world has never seen. Proximity to an ex-partner is closer than ever before.

Social media platforms are aware of this. After all, their function is to recreate interpersonal relations. The "relationship status" button was one of Facebook's first selling points. So, built into these mechanisms is also the option to erase someone. This can be indirect. For example, I recently went back to the message history between me and my ex and realized that there is no trace of a relationship there. All our photos have disappeared. Our text conversations have been wiped. Not a single memory to revisit. It's as if, in a way, my phone is telling me that it's time to be done with it.

But this can be direct as well. Social media allows you to unfollow, mute, restrict, and most severely, block someone you would no longer want to see on your feed. In the tumult of my breakup, I took the extreme route and blocked him on all platforms, opting to punish him for my pain. Once my anger had subsided a couple months later, I released the block—only to realize that the blocking function results in a total unfollowing of that person. Worse, when I visited his profile, I noticed he had deleted every picture of me. It was as if I had never entered his life to begin with. In the following months, the tumult started rolling again, and this time, in his words, it was his "turn to block me." Again, it was as if we had never existed to one another. We could live our lives in blissful ignorance. We could be post-zapped Mary's.

In many ways, it feels as though *Eternal Sunshine* predicted this current state of affairs. Digital life, for the most part, belongs to the past. With the exception of "live" videos, the digital world is an ephemeral archive, a collection of events, people, and things all sitting there, waiting for us to revisit them. This is in its very design. On Facebook, we scroll through "albums." Nowadays, my only use for the site is to dredge up old, cringey pictures to show to friends. Similarly, our iPhones bug us with "memories" from five, ten years ago, shoving our most awkward moments right in our faces. Instagram is the opposite—a curated page of the most aspirational times in our lives, to peacock the version of ourselves we'd like to immortalize. It's a mirror of real life, and also of our own inner worlds. But unlike either of these things, it allows, even encourages, us to forget each other.

In his exploration of the theme of memory in cinema, film and cultural critic James Bowman observes something about our society which nails down exactly why so many companies capitalize on our desires to erase each other, and maybe why memory loss is so pivotal to our daily lives that it's been transported onto our phones:

> We all instinctively feel that to lose our memory is to lose ourselves, a prospect that stirs audiences with mixed feelings…America is the land of second chances. We like to believe that history is bunk because we don't like being bound by it. Where fresh starts are a kind of national religion, and assuming that our other faculties remain more or less intact, memory-lessness is the ultimate fresh start.[41]

Forgetting is our cultural antidote for pain, and an elixir for moving into a brighter future. Like Mary, forgetting feels

*Eternal Sunshine: Auteur*

like the only option in a world where heartbreak is inescapable. Where memories are stitched into the fabric of physical and ephemeral life. Seeing an old photo or video of a past partner can be visceral. I've often felt a jolt of anger or the discomfiting buzz of anxiety when I stumble upon one. Now, I urge my friends who are going through breakups to block that person. "It's the best thing you can do to move on," I tell them. In this sense, I've been Clementine.

But I've also been Joel, realizing after getting dumped that I've been muted or blocked. That someone would choose to forget you can be a painful experience. But again, we consider it a necessary step towards healing. In regular grief, you do all you can to remember that person and to keep the image of them alive in your mind. In romantic grief, you have to *force* yourself to grieve. There is no ceremony, there are no rites. You must pretend that person never existed.

Yet as impressive as Dr. Mierzwiak's erasure technology may seem, even science can stumble. Once the truth about Mary's memory removal is revealed, it becomes clear that not even this innovative technology can reverse the teleological pull of true, everlasting love. Mary's passion for Dr. Mierzwiak is so strong that, memories or not, she finds herself drawn back to him. When the person you're trying to forget re-enters your life, erasure is futile. Perhaps we're all hard wired to find our way back to each other regardless of what's good for us. Her un-snuffable love is proof of Dr. Mierzwiak's fallibility.

Ten months after my breakup, I was on vacation in Greece when I received a message from an old university friend: "Did you guys break up?" A surge of panic overtook me, and I ran to the washroom, where I opened Instagram and scrolled as photo after photo from his birthday party appeared on my screen. It was the first birthday either of us was having since we had broken up, and the memories came crashing back. The feeling was hideous, and made even worse when logic kicked in and I put it together that he had posted an official photo with his new girlfriend, thus instigating a wave of messages from people who hadn't seen either of us in a while, asking if we had split.

Social media is an emotional landmine, disruptor of the healing process, and regressor of hard forgetting work. Since this incident, I've done the necessary blocking, muting, and restricting of any hidden bombs—mutuals who are still tangentially tethered, strangers I met through him, and of course, his own close friends. Yet every once in a while, something will slip through. Just recently, I was swiping through Instagram

*Eternal Sunshine: Auteur*

when I came upon a photo of him and his new girlfriend on a trip in Europe. This provoked yet another few weeks of tears and restless sleeps.

I was thinking of moving to New York—a city likened so often to Toronto, but one that could not be more different. Its historical flair, functioning subway system, and inconceivably vast expanse of brown, pre-war buildings have endowed a much-needed freshness into my life. We went to New York together five years ago. But at the time, we were both dead broke and in the midst of our cliched college drinking problems. My experience as a single twenty-six-year-old with a steady income will be, again, starkly different.

In Toronto, the specter of our relationship hides around the corner of Shaw and Queen Street West, along the sweeping stretch of Lake Ontario, in the thick musk of the City Pool bar, and the seductive funnels of Corona bottles. I hope that with a newfound and welcome anonymity, I will see nothing of him as I walk the streets. I will spend entire days completely alone, content with my new surroundings. I will embrace the loneliness. I will wrap myself around the resplendent nothingness of a life free from memory. I am happy with my procedure.

## Five: Filming The Spotless Mind

It was one of the coldest winters on record in New York, and Michel Gondry and his director of photography, Ellen Kuras, were preparing to shoot *Eternal Sunshine*. If Gondry was to strike his usual balance of naturalism and whimsy, he needed a DP with a similar eye. Kuras, whose background in documentary strikes its own balance of "raw and stylized imagery," was the ideal candidate.[42] So the two ventured out into the frigid New York streets in search of middle ground.

If it isn't evident by now, Gondry is a bit of a purist. Working with him is a pursuit of exaction, literalizing his vision to as sharp an outcome as possible. What proved difficult with this particular project though, was that *Eternal Sunshine* had a significant amount of unrealism in it. How is it possible to convey memory erasure in as natural a tone as possible? In the usual clashing of mind (director) and body (cinematographer), Kuras knew this would be an impossible feat. Her task was to fulfill three of Gondry's main requirements: to film only on practical location; to film only with available lighting (the

*Eternal Sunshine: Auteur*

lighting indigenous to a setting); and to execute all effects with only the use of a camera.

In Gondry's mind, all of this was nothing that the filmmakers of old hadn't done. Early European directors had conducted everything through analog means—allowing a single source to light an entire scene or simply shaking the camera to achieve a desired effect. That was cumbersome though. "Michel," pleaded Kuras, "even on a documentary, I wouldn't shoot exclusively with available light."[43] But practical was the vision, and so Kuras and her team compromised by hiding all sorts of regular lightbulbs behind the set pieces to "naturally" illuminate the scenes.

Their sparse use of lighting, while tedious in practice, succeeded in bringing together a very cohesive atmosphere to the film. Regardless of the tone or time of a given scene, the lighting feels lived-in. Daytime shots are subdued, with natural sunlight (or lack thereof) washing the characters over with a distinct frankness, which evoke lucidity. Some daytime memories are suffused with warm yellows—they are happier, more hopeful, and are usually during the brief moments where Joel and Clementine can speak candidly about their relationship.

Nighttime shots are quite different. The lighting is more

contained, almost glowing, always seeming to originate from nearby objects. Joel illuminated by the white-ish greens from passing storefronts, his face partially shadowed. Stan's face is lit from below with a small desk lamp, Mary by the warm glow of streetlamps. For the most part, it's naturalistic. But when Joel's memories begin to slip away, the lighting becomes harsher. A soft, yellow shot of the he and Clementine kissing under the covers quickly transforms into a closely lit shot of Joel scrambling to maintain his grasp under the sheets. The light is so close that his face is almost in vignette, as blackness slowly engulfs the frame.

These closely lit, heavily stylized shots appear during moments of mounting anxiety. In one instance, Joel and Clementine are lying on a bed of ice, illuminated in full by the cold glow of "moonlight." Joel says to Clementine, "I'm just exactly where I want to be." But in the next scene, they are transported abruptly to the floor of a busy subway station, a circular blue light aimed at the couple as people walk all around them, unphased. This is perhaps the most experimental sequence in the film in terms of lighting. Joel turns to Clementine, startled by their new environment, and then we cut to a shot of her lying on her side, staring at us in terror and lit starkly in cold blue as she is pulled backwards out of frame as if by a strong wind. Then a shot of legs walking, again in vignette. Joel, back on the ice, pleads with the sky to "call it off." Quickly, the memory-nightmare cuts and we jump back to Stan and Mary in warm yellows as they dance in their underwear over Joel's limp body. But then the memory resumes and Joel is on his knees on the ice yelling at the sky, his figure completely blown out by the light. The camera tracks him as he crawls helplessly along the ice crying out for Clementine, his face a white orb. "Joel-y!" she cries back, and he finds her lying on the ice. "We've gotta go," he says as he helps her up. The beaming white light follows, hunting them as they run away.

This stark lighting appears in another scene shortly after, when Joel and Clementine run out of a train station, as people around them begin to disappear, and into a winding hallway. The shots are almost completely black, except for a round, cold light on the subjects. Joel and Clementine hear a disturbance and turn to the hallway, and the light flashes over a memory of the couple playing jenga with some friends, the lighting so bright that memory-Clementine's face is briefly blown out. A circle of light passes over a frantic Joel and Clementine as they push further down the hallway, allowing their faces to fall into darkness as the light moves. They then find themselves in Dr. Mierzwiak's office, the light dancing across him as the camera pans to memory-Joel, then back to Mierzwiak, then creeping along the wall back to the Joel we entered the scene with. "Wake me up!" he screams. "Oh, I'm sorry Mr. Barrish. I thought you understood what was going on here," responds Dr. Mierzwiak pityingly. "You're erasing her from me. You're erasing me from her," says Joel, before turning around to find a faceless woman standing beside him. The beam is as pointed as ever, darting across the room as Joel grows more frightened by his distorted surroundings.

With its almost paranormal visuals, the scene plays out like its from a horror film. Gondry and Kuras achieved this lighting, what she referred to as the "memory-light," by attaching a small clip light to the camera, and then using a Par can light for wider shots.[44] This was a deviation from their typical reliance on available lighting, but its essence feels homemade, as though someone were standing behind the camera aiming a big flashlight at the actors. While the rest of the film is lit quite naturalistically, these more stylized scenes maintain their DIY quality. They unfold like a bad dream, one that is vivid but uncannily similar to everyday life, only slightly "off." As Kuras explains, "When you're remembering something, you don't get a full picture; you only see certain glimpses of the scene in your head, depending on what you're focusing on."[45] These sequences are nightmarish, but they are just sleepy enough to fuse seamlessly with the more lucid moments of the movie. In a way, *Eternal Sunshine* is a film watched with eyes half-open, its subjects and viewers both existing in a state of in-between.

Gondry's goal to execute the effects in the film with only a camera and clever visual trickery also reinforces the lived-in feel. In the director's words, "We decided early on that each time you see an effect in this movie, it has to give you a visceral response. You have to feel it."[46] Not a single traditional camera dolly was seen on set during production, as Kuras shot the entire film handheld. In the tradition of relying on found objects, Kuras used sleds as dollies, chariot dollies, and even wheelchairs when absolutely necessary. "The wheelchair dolly move wasn't always perfectly smooth," she said, "but there was often real beauty in that low-angle, wobbly movement, and I was willing to go with it."[47] In a strange way, practicality necessitates imaginative solutions like this.

Gondry puts his imaginative prowess on display in a number of ways. In the scene near the beginning of the film where Joel realizes Clementine has forgotten him, he steps away from her counter at the bookstore in disbelief. As he walks out, the industrial lights overhead switch off one by one with muffled pops like far-off gunfire as he steps through a doorway which leads into the living room of his friends' apartment. This clever camerawork gives the transition the weight it needs for us to understand Joel's disconnectedness, the way he has been drifting about, completely lost. Creativity also came in the form of building trick doors for the actors to run through as the scenery changes, and constructing oversized furniture, like the oversized tub they put Carry in to convey a bite-sized Joel bathing in his mother's sink.[48]

But practicality also necessitates very literal thinking. Shooting the majority of the film on location means shooting with what you have. If Joel and Clementine are chatting in a car, there is no process trailer to simulate the scene. Instead, Kuras and her team must pile into an actual car, with Carrey actually driving around, to get the shot. If Joel and Clementine are flirting on a train back from Montauk, the crew must hop on the train at a scheduled time and shuffle about the carriage as it hurdles along the tracks, trying to get the shot. For Kuras, this was no easy feat: "We only had a certain amount of time to get the scene. We had to use 1,000' mags to cover the scene in a oneshot deal, which is a killer way of shooting because you always have to be 'on.'"[49] As the camera reacts to its

*Eternal Sunshine: Auteur*

surroundings, jerking around in Kuras's hands, we as the viewer react with it. With every drop in the pavement or bump of the train, we feel like the weight of the environment and thus the story itself. We are effectively living in Joel's mind.

In what is arguably the emotional climax of the film, the time we've spent living in Joel and Clementine's world begins to peak. The couple find themselves in their earliest memory together, when they met in Montauk. They run towards a big house sitting on the beach and Clementine, brash as always, climbs through a window. Joel follows her in hesitantly, and we see that she is now holding a flashlight, its tiny beam darting across Joel's anxious face. The memory light finds us again, except this time it feels more gentle. We then cut to an exterior shot of the house falling apart, its shingles cascading to the ground. Back inside, Joel speaks to Clementine, both in voiceover and diegesis, "I've gotta catch my ride." "So go!" yells Clementine from upstairs, her voice echoing a bit. "I did," he says, looking up, "I thought you were a nut… but you were exciting." All the while, he is pacing around a pool of rushing water, foam unfurling from its edges, which has made its way into the house as the tide outside the window grows closer. By this point, the house is dotted with piles of sand. Its foundation crumbles around the couple as they kiss, completely unaware.

In this moment, we *feel* the gravity of their loss. Real sand and water encroaches on this tender, yet very painful memory. The actors look cold, and their characters' yearning for a warmer, wholler moment together exudes through the screen.

It was, in fact, real ocean water flooding through the house. Gondry's idea was to build a portion of the house right in the water. The goal was to wait for high tide so that it would roll closer up the beach, and then let the water overtake the set. But this would be one of many instances where Gondry's insistence on realness would clash with the people who worked for him:

> We hired a special team to put the set like two feet in the water. They had gear and stuff and then at the last minute they refused because they said it was too dangerous. So we were screwed, we had to do it ourselves - the actors, the producer, everybody—so I called them pussies I think. Then I got told off by the chief of the union, who came to sort of try to humiliate me in front of my crew because we fired those guys. I had my satisfaction![50]

An extreme commitment to realness can often result in

real problems on set. This is something Gondry's cast and crew came to learn as filming went on. He seems to detest all aspects of the film industry that suggest artifice. He believes that everything must be done to reflect life exactly as it is, as laboriously as possible, in dedication to the final product. Unions, which represent to Gondry the "industry" side of the industry rather than the artform, drive him crazy:

> I like to hire less people for my shoots, but in America the union forces you to work with too many people. There are rules that are absurd. For instance, I once wanted to shoot with local people who are not actors, but the SAG doesn't allow you to hire actors that are not in the union unless you also hire fifty people a day that are in the union. So we were shooting a dance scene and I had to hire not only dancers but also members of the SAG and the people from the union who were just extras acted literally retarded. They spent their day doing nothing, just looking at themselves in the mirror. All the older people had had plastic surgery. They just did a terrible job. There are so many rules with the union it is pathetic. I think that is very damaging for the American film industry.[51]

Of the actors Gondry did choose to work with, he made sure they would be cast so against-type that there was no room for them to *act*. Winslet, who rose to fame through a series of period dramas, most notably *Titanic*, was known for her serious, formal, and refined performances. Her casting as Clementine, uninhibited, erratic, and bold, could not have strayed further from this characterization. In the years following the film's release, Winslet has expressed a great deal of gratitude for the role. "I fought for the part, because it was a relationship movie that was different than any I had read," she told the *New York Times*. "And when I met Michel, I knew that he saw these characters as heroic and flawed and attractive and unattractive simultaneously."[52]

In a one-on-one discussion shortly after *Eternal Sunshine* was released, Winslet and Gondry sat down to talk about the film. As Gondry joins Winslet on the couch as she discusses her casting, he says, "We have to say the truth…that you were bitching about [the other women auditioning for the role]!" "I didn't bitch about anyone. That's fucking mean!" replies Winslet, smiling. Gondry laughs. "Well, we can't be nice to you. We have to get a good story out!"[53]

Gondry's greatest skill is working with what he has,

*Eternal Sunshine: Auteur*

manipulating his surroundings to extract their fullest potential. And just as he applies this tedious, analog process to the visual landscape of the film, he applies it to his actors as well. Gondry used an assortment of tricks to pull from his two leads a hint of truth in their performances. For example, he rarely yelled "action" or "cut" to bookend a scene. To the director, these words signaled to the actors to "turn it on" and begin a performance. Instead, he wanted a more fluid transition between the "off" and the "on" moments, to catch his actors off guard. "He liked creating that sense of confusion. He felt it was important for the movie," recalls Winslet.[54] On a traditional set, actors are designated their space to stand on camera with small pieces of tape on the floor called "marks." But Gondry ensured that marks were nowhere to be found. He also used a radio mic through which he communicated with both the actors and DP during a scene, meaning that they spent little time prepping or rehearsing a take before shooting. In a way, this afforded the actors a lot of creative freedom. As Winslet explains, "… it meant we could do the scene differently every time […] which meant that everything was very spontaneous and fresh in every take."[55]

The film is filled with fleeting scenes, woven together in a tapestry of bleeding colors. By Gondry's design, it's difficult to tell where one scene begins and the other ends. The memories are sutured in montage, with delicate, swelling music and whispers floating over the passing images. Winslet and Carrey appear entirely unaware of the camera in these moments. They seem to have developed special voices that their characters reserve for each other. Winslet's voice peaks in instances of affection, as does Carrey's. There is a lack of clarity in their delivery of lines, in the way a person who is very comfortable may mumble carelessly through their words. Or in the clipped, breathless nature a person who is feeling quite hurried may speak. It doesn't matter if a word is dropped here and there, because dialogue is secondary to emotion in this film.

Ultimately, Gondry's direction resulted in a very lived-in feel to the performances. The more natural an actor's performance, the more difficult a time they had on set. "I wanted everyone to be lost," he admits to Winslet. "Michel, trust me," she tells him, "everyone was as lost, if not more lost than you... have ever been in your life actually."

## Six: Jim and Joel

With a personal life kept very private, Jim Carrey's indomitable talent, charisma, and celebrity are instead reserved for the screen. But his comedic performances in *The Mask*, *Ace Ventura*, or *The Grinch* seem to spill beyond the screen's edges: larger-than-life, iconic, and so distinctly Jim Carrey. With the popular exception of *The Truman Show*, which hints at a slightly more subdued side of the actor, Jim's legacy is generally marked by those rubber-faced, over-the-top, and deeply physical portrayals of goofy characters. So, when Gondry, distaste for "actorly" actors not withholding, cast Jim in *Eternal Sunshine*, it would take a great deal of whipping in order to bring out his darker, more human side.

Following the release of the 2017 biographical documentary, *Jim & Andy*, which spotlights behind the scenes footage of Carrey's method acting on the set of *Man on the Moon*, the public would finally get to peek at the "real" Jim. He began speaking openly about his political opinions, spiritual beliefs, and experience with mental health. In an interview for the Toronto International Film Festival that year, he reflected on his struggles with depression, observing:

> People talk about depression all the time. And the difference between sadness and depression is sadness is just from happenstance, whatever happened or didn't happen to you. Grief or whatever it is. And depression is your body saying, "fuck you." I don't want to be this character anymore. I don't want to hold up this avatar that you've created in the world, it's too much for me.[56]

As is the case with many comedians whose personal lives are much darker than their public personas let on, Jim's combustible energy on screen scaffolds a more morose person within. This is part of what drew him to the role of Joel in *Eternal Sunshine*. For Carrey, it's the quiet tumult of the film's romance that packs the biggest punch: "It's romantic and yet not romanticized. It's a real love, full of compromise and everything else love comes with, rather than a *Romeo and Juliet* kind of movie."[57] And for Carrey, the emotional core of the film stems not from the idea of losing memories, but in being erased. When pushed about this further, he elaborates: "That was the strongest pull for me. That's a heavy feeling. That's what hit me with the script. When he finds out that she's erased him, it's just a brutal thing to hit probably anybody's ego, but a male ego especially."[58]

Here, Carrey is offering a profound resonation with, not only the character, but of a flaw, perhaps, in the male ego more generally. Joel is not so concerned with losing Clementine, but instead with a loss of a perceived miracle—that he would ever have entry into the life of someone he believes to be above him. The smallness of Carrey's performance renders for us a man who waits for the world to absorb him, rather than trying to absorb it himself. And through Clementine, someone whose life appears to be very big, who appears willing and eager to absorb all she can, Joel too can feel bigger, more interesting.

For over a decade, writers, critics, and public intellectuals have waxed on about Kaufman's critique of the "manic pixie dream girl" trope in *Eternal Sunshine*. Three years before Nathan Rabin ever coined the term in his 2007 review of *Elizabethtown*, Kaufman had already taken aim at this target. In what has become one of the most famous scenes in *Eternal Sunshine*, shared widely on Tumblr and the like, Kaufman wages his attack. Joel is following Clementine around the bookstore, as she walks about, disinterestedly re-organizing the shelves. He tells her he'd like to take her out, and she responds matter-of-factly, "you're married." "Not yet... not married," he says, shaking his head. Their conversation then proceeds as follows:

CLEMENTINE: Look man I'm telling you right off the bat, I'm high maintenance. So I'm not gonna tip toe around your marriage or whatever it is you've got going there. If you wanna be with me, you're with me.

JOEL: Okay.

CLEMENTINE: Too many guys think I'm a concept, or I complete them, or I'm gonna make them alive. But I'm just a fucked up girl who's looking for my own peace of mind. Don't assign me yours.

JOEL: [switching to present] I remember that speech really well.

CLEMENTINE: I had you pegged, didn't I?

JOEL: You had the whole human race pegged.

CLEMENTINE: Probably.

JOEL: I still thought you were gonna save my life. Even after that.

In the original script, just before Clementine launches into her "concept" speech, Joel tells her, "I just think you have some kind of... quality that seems really important to me." The use of the word "important" here suggests that, beyond having mere romantic or sexual appeal, Clementine has something innate to *offer* Joel. When Rabin wrote about Kirsten's Dunst's bubbly titular character in *Elizabethtown*, and Natalie Portman's Sam in *Garden State*, he was pointing to the trend of empty female characters who exist "solely in the fevered imaginations of sensitive writer-directors to teach broodingly soulful young men to embrace life and its infinite mysteries and adventures."[59]

What was and continues to be so irksome about the manic pixie is that she is not a fully realized character, nor a reflection of real woman, but rather a refraction of male ego. Often, she stands opposite to small, sad, or lost men, "thinkers," not unlike Joel, who will only crawl from the chambers of their own minds in pursuit of this impossible woman.

A cursory description of Clementine—whimsical, free-thinking, lustful, and addicted to box dye—would place her firmly into the "manic pixie" category. But, as so many have argued before me, *Eternal Sunshine* subverts that idea. While it predates its coining, the film is much more explicit in its attack on the manic pixie than something like *500 Days of Summer* which, for years, was misunderstood as a prime example of the manic pixie in action. The 2009 rom-com by Mark Webb follows a decidedly similar storyline, starting with a dissolution of the relationship between Tom and Summer, and then unraveling in a non-linear structure which recalls the higher points of the relationship, and where it went wrong. As Tom asks the viewer midway through, "Do you ever think about all the times you had with someone and you play it and look for the first signs of trouble?" *500 Days* also plays out like a memory reel, flickering through cheerful or saccharine montages of the couple's time together. Much like Joel and Clementine, the relationship begins with the man pleading with the woman to take a chance on him. Like Clementine, Summer is up front about her cynicism, warning Tom that she will not be able to give him all that he wants.

Initial readings of the film painted Summer as a

cold-hearted manipulator of "nice guy" Tom, but the film has since been redeemed as a critique of this male-centric assessment. *500 Days* is a litmus test for misogyny in the film viewing public as, over time, Tom has become a palpable antagonist—idealizing Summer in his mind as the ultimate woman, a free-spirit who will save him from the monotony of existence. His recountings of her are chopped up, sexy images of Summer lying in a bed of white sheets—perfect projections. When Summer falls short of his expectations, he quickly resorts to name calling ("skank" is a favorite) and listing all the parts of her he finds grotesque. Tom is not nice at all. He is often unlikeable, bombastic, and juvenile.

Over the course of the film, Summer becomes more human to us. She is less enthusiastic in their interactions. Her hyper-feminine 1950's garb becomes more modern. Her hair becomes less buoyant. In the third act, Tom's friends and acquaintances proclaim to the camera what their ideal partnership is. The less toxic of Tom's two friends, Paul, explains to us the girl of his dreams, then concedes that his current long-term girlfriend is *better* than that. Why? "She's real." The scene then cuts to an anguished Tom, trapped in a cycle of false memories haunted by a very "unreal" woman.

The final scene between Tom and Summer shows the

lovers sitting in their favorite spot on a park bench. Summer, going against all her initial heels-in-the-ground assertions about love not existing and casual dating, is now married. In response to Tom's disbelief, she tells him that she just woke up one day and knew. "Knew what?" he asks. "What I was never sure of with you." Tom now feels that all his romantic hopes were futile, that destiny is utter bullshit, and Summer assures him that if fate led her toward marriage, then maybe it will for Tom. He should not give up on his expectations. "It just wasn't me that you were right about," she tells him. The film ends with Tom attending a job interview where he meets the next girl of his dreams who, in the most obvious choice possible, is named "Autumn."

Beyond the standard misogyny of a 2009 viewing public, what I think contributed greatly to the film's initial misinterpretation is that Summer is quite an understated character—cool and collected, and performed with an uncharacteristic restrain by my YouTube namesake, Zooey Deschanel. Thus, Summer can easily be taken solely through the eyes of the audience surrogate, Tom, who only now has been reclaimed as unreliable. The polarized and ever-evolving reception of *500 Days* into the cultural consciousness is influenced by this lack of explicitness, a lack of insight into

Summer and her hopes and desires. Along with Tom, she is imperceptible to us, and can therefore easily be misunderstood as a manic pixie herself.

Conversely, if you were to look at the non-linear structure of *Eternal Sunshine* as beginning with the memory erasure, the reverse chronology of Joel's memories gives us a holistic depiction of Clementine. In the memory sequences, our perception of her replays from "difficult woman" as the two are nearing the end of their relationship, to "jovial free spirit" near the beginning of it. In this reading, having encountered Clementine first as the multifaceted person she really is, and then working in reverse to see her devolve into her more idealized form, the film complicates our understanding of her character before she ever utters the line, "too many guys think I'm a concept." This reading is a calculated unraveling of the "manic pixie."

Only, as we know, the film does not begin with Joel's memory erasure. It begins, instead, with him and Clementine, memories newly erased, meeting each other again in Montauk. A second first encounter. And in the choice to then begin and end the film with Clementine in her idealized form, Kaufman gives us yet another angle on the manic pixie. This one being that, often, after a breakup, we revert back to that vacant image.

In the two years following my breakup, I have spoken to a number of women who have expressed that, when exiting their own heterosexual relationships, they struggled to feel seen. That, in the eyes of their former partner, they often faded into the hollow outline of an "ex-girlfriend."

In my relationship, I was often the messier, more volatile, less affable one. Embarrassing him occasionally by instigating contrarian conversations with friends and reserving critical comments for the things he happened to enjoy. These conflicts would often end in him sighing and stating, "you're so… opinionated." Despite these moments of tension, our relationship was not *gendered*. He was not "the man" and I was not "the woman." In fact, sleeping in a bed every night, sharing meals, and allowing our work lives to overlap made it difficult to separate the lines between self and other. So, to me, the grief stemmed not only from losing someone I loved, but losing myself as well. This was something I cherished—that we were completely un-tetherable.

In our breakup, however, I felt I had become no more to him than "a woman," someone he could lament about to friends, acquaintances, and future girlfriends. Someone who had wronged him for ending the relationship, or who deigned to sleep with other people in the months that followed.

Or, the most difficult to cope with, someone who could be quickly replaced. After our most recent, ill-fated encounter at the birthday of a mutual friend, he called me on the phone to apologize for what had been a very strained interaction. "*I* feel like our connection supersedes all of this petty bullshit." I responded, "but it seems like you don't."

Me and the women in my life are utility for the men we date; we fulfill a purpose, be that guidance, nurturing, spiritual fulfillment, sexual gratification, or all of the above. And if *all* women are seen to have "that quality that seems really important," we are all dispensable. As I told him on the phone, I still struggle to find a semblance of what we had— that cosmic collision which, at that point in time, felt like it ruined my life. Whereas *he* struggled for a month or two, and then found a new me.

Like Joel, the men in my life jump from partner to partner, attempting to fill a sense of lack. This is what Clementine calls out in her speech, before proceeding to date Joel in spite of her better judgment.

*500 Days* ends with what reads as a pretty earnest message about fate, destiny, and hopeless romance. While Summer was not the girl Tom was right about, the film heavily suggests that Autumn most certainly is. *Eternal Sunshine*, on the other hand, does not have Joel moving onto a new girl, but rather ending up with the girl he was already with. Joel does not progress into the next season of his life. It is not up to the viewer, who has seen all parts of the character thus far, to decipher whether Clementine is a manic pixie. We know she is not. It is up to Joel to decide whether he will revert or not. His decision is unclear. And where Clementine is much more explosive and outwardly flawed than Summer, Joel is a shrinking violet next to the almost-cartoonish Tom.

Jim Carrey speaks with a degree of remove about the subjects he finds interesting. Depression is not "my depression." Ego is not, "my ego," it's "male ego." He disenfranchises himself from lived experience and instead looks at these subjects from the distance of a shrewd analyst. There is something deeply intelligent about the mask he wears in his films—an avatar which coolly satirizes the world around him and winks at the viewer from behind. As a result, tension arises when Jim is placed in an environment which does not allow him to think.

When Gondry watched Jim during the curtain call of the star-making early 90's sketch comedy series, *In Living Color*, he saw straight through the avatar. "On *In Living Color* they always go forward like *Saturday Night Live*," he recalled to

Charlie Rose, "but Jim is totally lonely and he is in the back. He is so charming. I have to call him and find out what's in his head."[60]

In *Eternal Sunshine*, Carrey had a hefty burden to bear playing Joel—a starring role which occupies a great deal of screen time, but functions as a passive observer to the action of the film. In his own words, "[Joel] doesn't have guile. He doesn't go into the world with a mask or a persona he carries."[61] The character, to a fault, is closed off and reserved, but beating inside him is an overwhelming sadness. This tension is completely internal, and thus nearly impossible to convey to viewers. Of course, Gondry took it upon himself to coerce it out of Carrey. "We had to trick him," recalls Kate Winslet in her discussion with Gondry. "Jim as a person is very alive and funny. Michel was always trying to keep him as contained as possible." Gondry balks at this. "I don't think I tried to contain him. I saw him on the set of another shoot when we were preparing and I saw him in between two takes… and I just realized in between takes he was a little bit different and he was really touching." Regardless of whether Gondry was *containing* Carrey's big personality or pulling out his sadness, the actors both agree that some trickery was involved in the process.

Whereas Carrey is now infamous for "going method" in *Man on the Moon*, being forced into someone else's method is something else entirely. Gondry's reliance on extracting authentic reactions from actors, or imposing physically taxing tasks upon them, did not exactly make him a friend to Carrey on set. In fact, the two repelled each other spectacularly. A scene where Joel and Clementine are soaking in the sink of Joel's childhood kitchen required the actors to sit in a tub for many hours. And Winslet, who seems to have found herself in water-related incidents on more than one set (see: *Titanic*), ended up fainting. When Gondry insisted on proceeding with the shoot, Carrey got angry. He told *Vanity Fair*, "People's nerves get frayed. Michel was going, 'Shoot, shoot!' and [Kate] was going, 'I'm nauseous.' And I got angry because she was not feeling well."[62] Gondry and Carrey proceeded to have a yelling match—which was not their first. When asked in the article what they did after wrapping the film, Carrey responds, "Michel and I had a fistfight in the street." The two have made up in the time since, and worked together on Dave Holstein's tragicomedy series, *Kidding*, in 2018. But Carrey's memories of *Eternal Sunshine's* production may need their own erasing.

Yet the scenes where Carrey felt duped into a good performance are arguably some of his best in the film. In one ,

*Eternal Sunshine: Auteur*

Mary begins to recite Pope's poem and we transition to shots of Joel and Clementine at an elephant parade. "It was the night the circus came into town," Carrey recalls in a behind the scenes featurette, "and we were down shooting some scene in the subway. And suddenly we just hear in the middle of everything, "THE CIRCUS! The circus is in town!"[63] Mary's poem flows into voiceover as sentimental music plays. The shots begin cutting abruptly from one to the other. "Of course, Michel doesn't think twice. That's the great thing, he just goes. And he said 'get in the vans!' And we're flying through town and we catch up to where the circus is gonna come around and all of us, crew, camera, everybody are running through the streets of New York."

In the rarest of instances, Jim reveals a bit of himself in Joel, as the character flings himself around, shirt overhead, wagging a sleeve around like an elephant trunk. Then a shot of Clementine on Joel's bag exclaiming, not unlike a child, "I want to be a great, big, huuuge elephant!" The camera pans over to the parade and a woman waves atop one of the elephants. Cutting back to the couple, Clementine is no longer there. By Gondry's design, Jim was not privy to Kate's disappearance. "That was one of my tricks," says Gondry, "I said, 'okay Kate go,'" and Kate ran away. In the scene, Joel's eyes are searching, his face is blank, as if the reality of her absence has not fully settled in. This is reflective of Carrey's overall performance in the film. He is often blank-faced and unawares. His emotions are subdued, and his speech is bumbling and incoherent. It is as far as possible from his appearances in films where he contorts his face to caricature-ish lengths and delivers his dialogue with an almost evangelical projection and cadence. With many of his real reactions caught by the camera, Carrey had no time to slip into the comforts of his on-screen persona. Reflecting on the scene Gondry said, "He looked so lost because you didn't have time to do the elephant trick, and we used this look in the film." Like Joel, Carrey's mask is stripped away, and what we are left with is a man unsure and deeply afraid.

At other times, however, Gondry demanded the full extent of Jim's acting prowess. "He comes in and asks me to do things that are impossible," Carrey recalls. In the scene where Joel's memory begins to glitch and he finds himself in a bizarro version of the Lacuna office, Carrey appears both as memory-Joel and present-Joel. The shot is blanketed in darkness, panning between present-Joel, who is flustered and panicking, and memory-Joel, who is sitting in a state of shock, about to sign off on the procedure. In Carrey's recounting of the shoot, he says:

*Eternal Sunshine: Auteur*

It's not split screen—it's not any of that—it's Michel coming in and saying [in a French accent], "You're going to run around the camera and you're going to put the hat on and take it off and put it on and take it off!" So, that's me going back and forth behind the hand-held camera in the dark. I'm not kidding. That's what was happening in that scene. It was just about how quickly can you run through the dark, get a jacket and a hat on and then completely change your attitude to the person on the other side of the room. And I argued with him. I said, This can't be done. I can't do this. It's impossible." He said [in a French accent], "How do you know if you don't try?[64]

The result is deeply compelling. Memory-Joel is ashen-faced. His eyes are glued to the floor, nerves pulsing in his temples. When the camera whips back to present-Joel, Carrey has traveled into another dimension of feeling in the span of mere seconds. Tears are glinting in the corner of his eyes. His brow is furrowed and his eyes are glazed, as if he just took off a pair of glasses. He cowers at the door, breathing deeply and looking frenzied. The range that Gondry pushed out of him in this scene is enough to cement Carrey as one of the Greats, and cements *Eternal Sunshine* as the ultimate inversion of the manic pixie.

What works so well about Carrey's candid performance is that it underscores what so fundamentally resonated about the character—that Joel is not active, he is reactive. Again, he is driven not by the desire to erase, but by the fear of *being erased*. And Carrey's self-awareness, coming together with Kaufman's foresight and Gondry's emotionality, make for a now pioneering indictment of a trope that had not even been invented yet. The Joel we are given is cowardly, tender, oblivious, and maybe even dull. The mask is torn off and Carrey is stripped to his most naked self—the male ego, shrinking at the force of a woman much fuller than it could ever comprehend.

## Seven: Fade To White

As our lovers run up the wintry Montauk beach, little dark blobs disappearing into blinding snow, we are not pulled into the comfort of blackness often expected from the ending of a film. Rather, we are left with a *white* screen.

Before this, Joel and Clementine are standing in the hallway, dancing back and forth: "You will think of things! And I'll get bored with you and feel trapped because that's what happens with me." "Okay" he shrugs, smiling. "Okay" she breathes. Before that, they are standing in the bookstore, where Joel pleads, "It'll be *different*, if we could just give it another go around."

In one version of Kaufman's script, *Eternal Sunshine* had a much darker ending, with Joel walking away from Clementine. In another version, it's revealed that the story has been taking place in Clementine's mind the entire time. Both of these options leave us with a very different take away than the one we are ultimately given. The first prescribes a lesson onto the viewer—that this relationship was toxic, primarily for Joel, and that his decision to leave is a sign of growth, and that he now understands some fundamental flaw in the relationship and must act accordingly. The second tells us that Clementine is either clinically unwell, or (the more likely case) that she has been envisioning a scenario wherein she erased Joel from her mind, and she is weighing out the impact of this choice. Yet neither of these endings is the one we got. In the words of Yohanna Desta, "Gondry's relatively happy ending won out instead."[65] But is *the ending happy*? As we, the viewer, sit with this cold white image, we are left to wonder whether Joel and Clementine have entered into bliss, or a terrifying unknown.

If we take a glance at the endings of two other major romance films that came out the same year as *Eternal Sunshine*, *The Notebook* and *Before Sunset*, both of which are concerned with ideas of love and memory, perhaps we can better understand this question.

*The Notebook* is about a man and a woman working together, in the later stages of the woman's dementia, to recover and preserve her waning memories of their decades-long romance. Once the memory of their love is recovered for a final time, the two die happily in their sleep, holding hands.

Rickard Linklater's *Before Sunset* is a bit more realistic. It's about two people, Celine and Jesse, who, after a chance encounter, spend nine years apart building separate lives, before finding their way back to each other. The film's ending is heavily suggestive—Celine is dancing to Nina Simone's "Just in Time" as she and Jesse exchange a knowing smile from across the room. "Baby, you are gonna miss that plane," Celine says, quoting the lyrics to the song. "I know," Jesse replies.

What do these endings have in common with *Eternal Sunshine*? How do they differ? Well, *The Notebook* tells the story of an epic romance—one with great social and cultural forces pulling the two lovers apart. Their commitment to remembering one another allows their love to triumph. *Before Sunset* is more grounded in its romance, but again, the obstacles standing in the way of the lovers are tangible—distance, time, trains, flights, sons, wives and grandmothers. As is the case with so many romances, if all the world fell away, these two people would be together. Of course, *Before Sunset's* 2013 follow up, *Before Midnight*, would challenge the assumption that these lovers were made for one another—but as Celine and Jesse smile in that Parisian living room in 2004, we, and they, are none the wiser.

Unlike these literary and filmic descendants of *Romeo and Juliet*, there are no external forces pulling apart the lovers in *Eternal Sunshine*. Rather, their internal makeup, their hardwiring, is incompatible. *They* are what pulls them apart. And so, rather than holding onto their memories, they work quickly to be rid of them. Unlike the storied romance, *Eternal Sunshine* is neither epic in scale, nor particularly virtuous in its end. Rather, if you dig through the layers of white snow, you'll find a discomfiting verisimilitude in the message it leaves behind.

When my relationship ended, there were no external forces pulling us apart. My parents loved him, his parents loved me. We continued to make each other laugh. We were both upwardly mobile in our careers. After much tumult, we finally lived in the same city. And yet, premonitions about our demise started creeping into my mind about two years before it happened. The reasons were rather mundane—I was young! I needed to gain life experience! I needed to learn real independence! I voiced this to him a few times, and he agreed. Yet none of these reasons felt valid enough to pull us apart. So, when our relationship ended, we told ourselves that "in five years, we'll find our way back to each other again." When we were breaking up, and multiple times in the months that followed our breakup, we affirmed to one another that we were soulmates, but this was just not our time. Naively, we thought that the future, with its wisdom, would be.

Gondry considers himself a pessimist, as his earlier quote in this book about Björk makes clear—"Once, I was talking to Björk, and she said to me, 'You're the most pessimistic person, but at least you're funny.' And I think that's something you could say about Charlie, as well."[66] It is therefore a possibility that his choice to close on a white screen was an ominous one.

Let's revisit the ending. Clementine and Joel are mulling around Joel's living room, listening to the tape. Joel asks, "You want a drink or something?" and Clementine responds, "Do you have any whisky?" Joel's voice plays on the tape, full of malice: "*I saw it clearly the last time we were together. It wasn't sexy, it was just sad.*" Clementine looks baffled as the tape lashes on: "*The only way Clem thinks she can get people to like her is to fuck them. Or at least dangle the possibility of getting fucked in front of them. I mean she's so desperate and insecure, that she'll sooner or later go around fucking everybody.*" Crestfallen, Clementine objects. "I don't do that," she says. "I wouldn't think that about you," he says. "Because I don't." "I know!" "Because it really hurts me that you said that because I don't do that." Orchestral strings play and Clementine excuses herself. She walks out the door and into the hallway. "Wait!" cries Joel. Clementine whines, "What do you *want* Joel?" "Just wait! I don't know, I want you to wait for just a … while." Long pause. Clementine looks at him with a mixture of fear and surprise. He bites his lip. She begins to cry and the camera becomes slightly more unstable, less focused. "Okay."

The scene changes and washes over the beach with a cold blue hue, our two atoms bouncing around its expanse. Beck begins to moan, "change your heart," and then the shot jump cuts and pulls the lovers back to us before they run away again. The verse restarts, "change your heart." A cycle repeating.

If there are no existential reasons for why Joel and Clementine should terminate their relationship, there is nothing truly stopping them from getting together again. Yet, we've seen what this relationship has turned them into. We are given evidence of it right before the white screen appears. They themselves have seen what they will become, but they move forward anyway. Some view this as a tragedy—two people doomed to repeat their own misery. But there is room for a happier ending.

In a time where dating apps seem to dominate the romantic landscape, it is difficult to find space for mess or imperfection. I myself have experienced my share of what I like to call "logic dumpings," where I am the unwilling subject of an unceremonious termination to a relationship, as the other person regales me with what can only be defined as "therapy speak."

Up until the moment in which I was dumped, I had believed these situations to be moving along quite well—only for it to end abruptly, justified with vague, new age reasonings. It was like having a doctor's note shoved into my hand with a list of platitudes like "work on myself" or "not ready" scribbled over it. In the past, I would accept a person's inability to pursue a relationship due to their own emotional turmoil as fair, or even healthy. But at the tail end of these dumpings, I found myself asking whether we are too often opting for the logical route, severing ourselves from our hearts in the process.

I fear that love and logic may overlap more than necessary these days. The emergence of dating apps has encouraged a fine-tuning process, cracking at the mold of a person optimized just for us, or at least a person we envision on paper. There is no happenstance, no chance, no risk. We filter away all the "red flags," and are left with the ostensible love of our lives—all before the first date. When I hear stories of how the parents of my generation got together—meeting as coworkers, a chance encounter on a flight, leaving partners for each other—it all sounds very imperfect. Is there a line between perfection and toxicity? Perhaps love is about finding the ideal point on the line which preserves our own wellbeing, while giving us room to be human. Logic brings comfort and safety, but does it necessarily bring happiness?

After two years of being single, I find myself yearning for someone to take a risk on me the way Joel and Clementine take a risk on each other. I am open to love and all the pain that comes with it.

This risk-driven reading of the film sees the white screen as blissful. Joel and Clementine have chosen love. Not the pure love of other romance films, but a love that cannot be tarnished by the world it exists in, one with an eternal shelf life. In this reading, Joel and Clementine's love is impure and difficult, but it is triumphant.

Gondry was once told that his movies "have utopian elements in them."[67] When asked if he himself believed in utopia, he answered:

> Yes. I actually have proof of that, because I tried systems that were not supposed to work but they did. For example my mother was very badly addicted to Codeine, which is like opium but you can find it in some over the counter medicines. She was addicted to the point that she was going to die. So I went to her pharmacist and showed her a picture of my mom and

told her that she can't sell these drugs to her anymore. The pharmacist told me that it is illegal not to sell this product to her because you don't need a prescription. So I told her: "Fine so she will be dead and you will be responsible for it." She felt guilty and stopped selling it to her. That was enough to stop my mom. I didn't even have to go to other pharmacies. We walked out of the system. People think that we are not in position to create a system but I think that is wrong. Everybody can create a system that works.

When considering this anecdote in conversation with the film, it seems that Gondry has a utopian take on the ending of *Eternal Sunshine*. Joel and Clementine spend the entire film dodging the memory removal machine, evading a system which seeks to "logic" love out of existence. The memory removal process lays waste to love's imperfections by offering its participants a "spotless mind." Against all odds, and the odds of their own choices, Joel and Clementine choose a system that works for them—one that may bring them misery, but which sees love as the victor.

As in life, the white screen leaves us no answers—which is the true accomplishment of *Eternal Sunshine*. When I think back to my breakup, I still do not know if it is true that in five years, three now, we will find our way back to each other. Both versions of the future, one with him and one without, disturb me. The future is open and empty; there is nothing to read. Only white.

## Eight: You, Me, And Our Favorite Movie

*Eternal Sunshine* has been described as a cult classic. (It's even listed as such on the film's Wikipedia entry.) But when considered with the publicly accepted definition of a "cult film," it is not immediately clear why this is the case.

In the time-honored tradition of film scholarship and genre classification, no one can agree on what exactly "cult" cinema means. Film scholar Elena Gorfinkel is of the camp which views cult cinema as a distinctly physical phenomenon which had its heyday in the B-movies (movies that were both commercial *and* critical flops) of the 1960s and 70s. Audiences, often cast out of dominant society, would empathize with these films, which were themselves culturally outcasts for their low culture sensibilities. And thus, "bad taste" films like *The Rocky Horror Picture Show*, *Robot Monster*, *Plan 9 From Outer Space*, and *Showgirls* became film-viewing events which took on entirely new lives after their initial releases, embraced by raucous audiences who would congregate in the cinema to belt out their favorite quotes in unison, dress up in costumes, and throw popcorn at the screen. "The efflorescence of the midnight-movie circuit in the early 1970s, in urban locales like the Elgin Theater in New York's Chelsea neighborhood as well as in college towns," writes Gorfinkel, "seemed to shift the field, from the 'death of the author,' to the (re)birth of the audience."[68]

But times change. And as digitization and streaming slowly erode the cinema, so too does the importance of physical locale. "It seems," Gorfinkel postulates, "that the cultist and the cinephile have in the present become indistinguishable from each other, through the overlaps between their broadening span of tastes and the way that technological, rather than geographical, spaces have afforded or delimited such widening."[69] For Gorfinkel, the cult film not only hinges upon physical locale, but *also* its low culture. Due to this distinction, Gorfinkel makes a hard line between cinephiles, who consume film for the sake of art, and cultists, who consume it for the sake of trash.

*Eternal Sunshine* is certainly not "trash." While it wears an inside aesthetic that sometimes signifies low production value, it is also clear that a great deal of thought went into the film. A perfunctory look at *Eternal Sunshine* should tell the viewer that what they are watching is crafted by people with significant expertise in their respective fields. Kaufman's writing is intricate and winding, his themes gently couched within realistic dialogue. His words pack an emotional punch—all the hallmarks of a good writer. *Eternal Sunshine* is also largely considered one of Kaufman's more palatable movies for its universal themes and compelling arcs

The acting is similarly award-worthy in its nuance. While the direction is innovative and heavily stylized, it never feels like it's attempting to overpower the story at its core. With all of this considered, along with its decent budget and favorable critical response, we would be remiss to place it within the B-movie category.

Instead, the movie fits much more neatly into J. Hoberman's conception of the cult film. In a critical symposium on cult cinema, Hoberman offers a very different reading from Gorfinkel's, arguing that not all cult films align with the B-movie classification of low culture excess and controversy. Rather, he says, "some cult films—say *Blade Runner*—were commercial flops that gathered enthusiasts over a period of time."[70] This class of cult movie is one that was made with the intention of reaching a wide audience, but falls short of that goal—instead enjoying a delayed response, or renaissance, years later.

This dampens the "trash" element of Gorfinkel's definition and expands it to include cinephiles as well. And if we are to understand *Eternal Sunshine* as being quite sophisticated in its budget and formal filmmaking techniques, the movie belongs more to the latter camp.

And bridging together Hoberman's definition with Gorfinkel's is their privileging of the audience as the indicator of what makes a film "cult." Where Gorfinkel views the "(re) birth of the audience" as core to this phenomenon, Hoberman similarly argues that it is the audience's remaking of it.[71] For Hoberman, the transformation of a cult film is bottom-up, a process which is "essentially democratic—anti-supply side and, in some respects, antiauthoritarian."[72] Whether it is a sensorially abrasive B-movie or a big budget studio misfire, the film becomes cult through a process of audience fetishization. For *Eternal Sunshine* to be considered a cult classic, it did not have to become a midnight event, or even so monumental a flop. Rather, it had to be absorbed as something integral to audience identity.

In the same cult cinema symposium, Tim Lucas notes that "today's cult movies are generally watched in solitude by cultists who connect through magazine articles, blogs, and message boards."[73] What he is referring to here is that, in the two decades since *Eternal Sunshine's* release, digitization, and now the advent of streaming, have completely shaken the structures of film consumption. This is viewed by many as a death knell for the cult film—a perspective which posits that the entrapment of film within the four walls of our computers, tablets, and smartphones has individuated the viewing experience and thus undermined the sense of community that is understood as integral to cult cinema.

But if we are to privilege Hoberman's definition of cult and exclude the locale argument, then the individual viewing experience, the exodus of cinephiles and cultists from the theater to blogs and message boards, may actually enhance audience fetishization. For Hoberman, the cult film can serve both roles, it can "confirm individual identity, as well as serving to establish and define a particular community."[74]

I posed a series of questions to my followers on X (about forty of them) to get a sense of their relationship to *Eternal Sunshine*. A significant portion who responded had discovered the film through social media. Of those who had found the film in this way, many seemed to have been drawn to it initially on an aesthetic level. One person specified that they had seen screen caps of the movie online and then watched it *because* they "liked the quotes and the aesthetic." Several had found it on specifically image-based platforms like Instagram and Tumblr:

> A child of Tumblr in my teens, I had seen several snippets, shots, and quotes from the film which piqued my interest. When I realized I recognized and liked most of the cast, I streamed it online and really loved it.

> In the early to mid 2010s, I was starting to get into indie film. While browsing Tumblr one day, I saw some gifs from *Eternal Sunshine*. The images I saw just perfectly piqued my interest.

Others had it recommended to them by a YouTuber:

> This was […] the same year I discovered bestdressed (I miss her), and she made a video called "geeking out about movies for 24 minutes straight." One of the movies she listed was *Eternal Sunshine of the Spotless Mind*.

As streaming individualizes the movie-viewing experience,

we turn our identifications with film inwards. The social cataloging site, Letterboxd, which has become an ephemeral town square for cinephiles, is evidence of this internalization. Letterboxd's interface is designed to optimize audience customization, comprising a variety of features which encourage its users to orient their own individual film identities. These features include: watchlists; paid memberships; typified lists like "Befriending the lyrical loneliness" and "sigma but women;" audience movie reviews; and a feature on each profile page which allows users to display their top four favorite movies to friends.

*Eternal Sunshine* is wildly popular on Letterboxd. At the time of writing, it has 2.1 million watches, appears on 313,000 lists (including "Befriending the lyrical loneliness" and "sigma but women," as well as my personal favorite, "Psychosexual dramas, nihilistic fever dreams & surrealism with a touch of humor,") has been liked by 878,000 users, and has an overall rating of 4.2 by 88,000 fans. When comparing these numbers to similar films discussed in this book, like *500 Days of Summer* and *Before Sunrise*, *Eternal Sunshine's* online popularity is staggering. (A majority of the people who answered my questionnaire on X—78 percent to be precise— had a Letterboxd account, with an even greater majority—89 percent—answering that they would put *Eternal Sunshine* in a list of their favorite movies.)

In this online lexicon, "cult" takes on a new meaning. No longer is it only the audience redemption of an outcasted or overlooked film, but also central to the identity of the individual person who views it. In an era where social media has increasingly become a space for curating and typifying our identities based on the media we consume—a gallery of icons, photos, and thumbnails which present a version of the self we would like to be—so too does our approach to movies. "Letterboxd Top Four" is now an identification tool used to form online friendships and seek common ground on dating apps. "Ladies", the internet tells me, "if his favorite movie is *Fight Club*, run for the hills. If she loves *Shiva Baby*, you may proceed without caution!"

For a long time, *Eternal Sunshine* was one of my top four films on Letterboxd—along with *Muriel's Wedding, The Devil Wears Prada*, and *Kuch Kuch Hota Hai*. This was until I took them all down for fear that their posters were ugly. Which is ironic given that Michel Gondry was happy with *Eternal Sunshine's* poster and once said this:

A lot of times, people say, "But nobody will judge a

film based on the poster." I get so offended when I hear that. I'm like, "If you don't care about what goes on the poster, then let us do it, because we do." To me, the poster for *Human Nature* is hideous. The guy who decided to do this image, especially for the DVD, I made him promise to apologize to me after the video came out and didn't rent well. Because he promised me it would be a success.[75]

The *Human Nature* poster *is* hideous—Arquette, Robbins, and Ifans are cut out and pasted crudely onto a cloudy white background under a slime green title. *Eternal Sunshine's* poster is certainly an upgrade. Carrey's face is larger than the image of he and Winslet, providing the image a greater degree of depth. Behind the figures is a sheet of ice, a great crack running between Carrey's head and the two lovers, a double visual for the breakages in Joel's mind as well as the cracks forming in his and Clementine's relationship. The orange title font is simple and elegant. Yet it also has the distinct quality of a 2000s comedy poster—perhaps its the deep saturation, or the roundedness of the font, or Carrey's expressive eyes. And this, shallowly, cheapened the look of my top four list. (I now have a set of more secondary, "intellectual" movies in my Letterboxd top four in the hopes that they present a more refined version of myself to whoever visits my profile.) Yet while *Eternal Sunshine's* poster did not align with my tastes on an aesthetic level, I still embrace the film as an integral part of my own identity.

Hearing from people on X, I got the sense that *Eternal Sunshine* is a very personal film for many. Some mentioned its rewatch-ability, unusual story structure, or evocative visualization of memory as reasons why the film had such an impact. But while these concern the filmmaking, the most recurring trend in the responses was the way *Eternal Sunshine* became enmeshed as a facet of the self, providing catharsis and provoking a powerful release of emotions:

> I remember uncontrollably crying in my high school bedroom for the last 20 minutes of it, stifling my sobs so I wouldn't wake my parents. I think I'm definitely more aware of the real life implications of the "manic pixie dream girl" trope because of Clementine. I'm also a self-admitted hopeless romantic desperately clinging onto the hope that real love is worth suffering for and I feel like *Eternal Sunshine* has only exacerbated that fact as I've gotten older.

The film can also be a soothing comfort in moments of hardship:

> It struck a chord with me while I was going through a really hard time in my life (and just beginning to study college in film no less!) and pushed me towards appreciating more introspective, personal movies.

> It was the first movie I remember watching that truly impacted me on an emotional level that I wasn't able to fully grasp or understand. I think this movie has given me a lot of peace in hard times.

Some felt that the relatability of the film's characters and situations made them less lonely, the same way it made me feel during my breakup:

> When I was in my late teens, I went through my first breakup. All I wanted to do was consume books and tv shows/movies that contained sad stories. By that point I understood *Eternal Sunshine* to be a breakup movie, so I went to my local video store to rent the

DVD. I even watched it on a Valentine's Day because that's when the opening of the movie takes place, so I maybe I would feel less alone in my raw emotions.

I watched it as a freshman in college during a pretty sad/lonely period and definitely related to Joel. I also just thought it was brilliantly constructed. It had a very precise tone. The blended/nonlinear narratives were smart. The themes were relatable. I loved the score/soundtrack. To me, when you're that age, films or musicians can really click with you and feel very personal, like you're the only one who GETS it. *Eternal Sunshine* was one of those movies for me.

A great number of people told me that the film inspired hope in them, that Joel and Clementine's decision to get back together at the end was a sign that risks are worth taking:

I love that it's desperate and hopeful at the same time. I relate to both Clementine and Joel in different ways, how much I do varies year to year as I grow up. The ending makes me cry harder than almost anything. I think it's one of the most romantic movies I've ever seen, at least my definition of romance.

i rewatch it every valentine's day. it made me feel a depth of emotion i don't think i'd really ever experienced before from a piece of art. i really love how it examines its central relationship and the idea that experiencing love is worth it even if a relationship ends badly. i saw a lot of myself in clementine and how she approaches love.

For one person, it was even an instructional tool:

This movie, believe it or not, has prepared me for relationships. I hadn't had much luck with love and connecting with people. I've always felt too uncomfortable and too afraid of heartbreak to try but *Eternal Sunshine* tells me that they are worth that risk. They may cause hurt, and you may not like yourself at the end of them, but the love and companionship they bring are necessary. When Clementine tells Joel their relationship is doomed to fail again Joel just says "Okay." I always want to cry at that.

*Eternal Sunshine* did not only inspire taking risks on romance, it also contributed to people taking risks with self-expression:

> For one, I dyed my hair a vibrant color (purple) that I would desperately like to have again. But another think this movie did was encourage me to be the person who speaks first. Or if I've been too scared to talk to people, I've written letters to people to introduce myself. The letter thing always blows up in my face, but I have had some success with making friends where I was the one who said hi first.

> I think it might've kicked off my interest in quiet brunette men who look sad, also my need to be looked at the way Joel looks at Clementine. I also own multiple fur coats and dye my hair orange about once a year thinking delusionaly that this time it'll suit me. Beyond that I think it's probably fundamental to who I am and view love in a way I can't articulate because I saw it at such a formative age I don't know what I would've thought if I hadn't.

i'm an aspiring filmmaker and i credit eternal sunshine as one of the films that awakened that passion and made me understand the power of the medium. i also really love clementine and i've picked hair colors that match hers a few times (and bought an orange hoodie lol).

Most impressively, the film has such an impact on some people as to change the course of their lives. For example, it set this person on their career path:

It was one of the first scripts that I downloaded and read. It reaffirmed my desire to be a writer. The Script made me realize that there can be much more to a Love Story, that a perfect balance between simplicity and complexity can be reached, and that love impacts us in more ways than just not being lonely.

And it even influenced this person's worldview:

I'm not exaggerating when I say this film is responsible for a lot of my views on what it means to be a person. Watching Joel desperately try to cling on to his memories is my reminder to remain grateful for my own experiences of love, even in the face of loss and heartbreak. Everything we experience is what makes us who we are, and I know i'm due for a rewatch when I catch myself being cynical about it.

It became clear from these responses that there are several reasons why *Eternal Sunshine* went through a process of audience fetishization (and thus became a cult classic). The biggest reason being the internet. The film's unique visual language and wistful dialogue lends itself well to decontextualization—allowing the movie to be spliced and transformed into images that are then spread online. Visually pleasing images accompanied by poetic lines like, "blessed are the forgetful" and "I can't remember anything without you" have populated image-based platforms for over a decade now. It's also a deeply felt film with a universal emotional resonance (who hasn't felt regret, or heartbreak, or longing?) Together, these attributes give the film a lasting power that has translated seamlessly into the age of aestheticization. As we fold the media we consume into who we are, and then showcase who we are to the world, *Eternal Sunshine* becomes us.

In a now seminal 1985 essay on cult film as it relates to

*Casablanca*, Umberto Eco pondered the cult transformation process, theorizing that, "I think in order to transform a work into a cult object one must be able to unhinge it, to break it up or take it apart so that one then may remember only parts of it, regardless of their original relationship to the whole."[76] When assessing Eco's words within the full history of cult cinema, it can be argued that through the process of fetishization, audiences repurpose a film they love either for their specific communities, for their own individual identities, or both simultaneously.

This may be the exact reason that I've had different readings of *Eternal Sunshine* at different times—absorbing the film into my own identity and thus allowing it to transform as my identity did. I am a woman in love; this film is about love. I am a woman experiencing grief; this film is about grief. In my disparate readings I disjointed parts of the film from their greater whole, and now that it is within me, I can no longer look at it as a whole, but rather in fragments of feeling. Anyone who wants insight into who I am must understand my love for this film.

This is why, when someone I recently went out with told me on our first date that his favorite movie was *Eternal Sunshine*, I was overjoyed. Taking this as a "green flag," any reservations I had about our compatibility were nullified, and I proceeded "without caution." Until, when I recounted this to my friend, she said "Are you sure about that? Sounds pretty *basic* to me." This puzzled me. How could a film which has been celebrated for its alternative appeal be considered basic, mainstream?

The people who answered my questionnaire were also divided on this. When asked whether they thought *Eternal Sunshine* was a cult film, some agreed, but for varying reasons. To my relative surprise, many responses expressed the idea that *Eternal Sunshin*e is an underrated film:

> Yes, I think it is. I have not seen enough people talking about it [and I] would love to see if many people were aware of this film.

While it remains unclear as to whether *Eternal Sunshine* is indeed underrated, this understanding of "cult" is in keeping with the general, traditional definitions of the term I outlined earlier. But other respondents who agreed offered differing understandings of what a "cult" film was to them. Some argued that *Eternal Sunshine* is cult because it has a timeless quality to it. For others, the film is cult because it pushed technical or thematic boundaries. Many argued that *Eternal Sunshine* is a cult film because it is well-liked by the general public. Interestingly, some said the opposite—that *Eternal Sunshine* is cult because it has a distinct audience. Who this audience is differs from person to person:

For a subgroup. Like very 500 days of summer, Her, stale white boy and manic pixie dream girl film bros.

Or (my favorite) the romantically bereaved:

I'm not sure I would call it a cult classic, even though I personally came to know about it in kind of a "cult" /unconventional way. I get the sense that the cult of fans of *Eternal Sunshine* is a cult largely made up of people who've had their heart broken /have broken someone's heart, but.... you know what? I guess I would call it a cult classic.

However, if the movie's universal appeal also stems from its portrayal of heartbreak, then can the audience be cult? This is where we arrive at the divide. Most people expressed that the film is "too successful" to be cult. This person argued that the fan base was *too* universal:

> No. I wouldn't say cult classic because I don't think there's a specific fanbase for it or type of person that enjoys it. It's just an amazing film some people have either seen or they haven't.

The film was too popular with the general public for some:

> I think a cult classic would have to be more rarely seen than I perceive *Eternal Sunshine* to be, but maybe that's my fault for running in movie loving circles.

And it enjoyed too much mainstream success when it came out:

> I'm not sure if I would actually. I think "cult movie" has a completely different meaning than it did 20 years ago. I think *Eternal Sunshine* is just a little too known for cult status. It had mainstream success, I think it won an Oscar, and it is one of the most popular movies in internet spaces like Letterboxd.

For this person, *Eternal Sunshine's* prevalence online, especially on sites like Letterboxd, was the very reason why it cannot be considered a cult classic:

> A few years ago maybe, but now I think [it] is a pretty well-known movie. Is almost on every must-watch list on Letterboxd, and it was mentioned multiple times on my run of film school.

So it appears my friend and I are not the only ones to have opposing opinions about *Eternal Sunshine's* legacy. The film dodges clear answers within the zeitgeist as to how it was made, how it was received, the type of audience its gained, and what sort of "vibe" it's emitting to viewers. It provides no answer as to why I find its poster ugly. One person noted this gray area of classification:

> I would consider it somewhere between a regular classic of the 2000s and a cult classic. It was a financial success, but I think it's [sic] charm certainly lies in an indie canon rather than a mainstream one. With a writer like Kaufman, a score from Jon Brion, and a disorienting sentimentality sort of adverse to

the typical narrative of a rom-com, it feels more independent despite how performed [sic] at the box office.

How can one film be fetishized by a niche audience, and be universally beloved? Successful upon release, yet under-rated? Boundary-pushing, yet mainstream? Well, much of this cultural mystification can be attributed to how *Eternal Sunshine* was marketed.

## Nine: Selling the Spotless Mind

*Eternal Sunshine* is a film which very much straddles the line between high and low culture. For some, myself included, it's a moody, atmospheric arthouse movie. For others, like my friend, it's a quirky rom-com.

The trailer, for instance, is enough to dupe audiences into believing that they're about to watch another mid-2000s fluff piece. It begins with a grainy commercial for Lacuna Inc. (which never appears in the film) delivered by Dr. Mierzwiak, his face then splitting into moving grids. "Hello, I'm Howard Mierzwiak, founder and president of Lacuna Inc. Why remember a destructive love affair? Here at Lacuna, we have perfected a safe, effective technique for the focused erasure of troubling memories. In a matter of hours our patented non-surgical procedure will rid you of painful memories and allow you a new and lasting peace of mind you've never imagined *possible*." The moving grids then disappear with the sound of a shot blasting. Cut to Carrey leaning forward in his seat at the Lacuna office. He asks, "this is a hoax, right?"

What we get from the trailer that follows is an air of comedy. Electric Light Orchestra's upbeat "Mr. Blue Sky" is the song of choice—the bass bouncing along as the grids appear and disappear from the screen—with credits playing in the style of a sitcom (name appears, actor makes a wacky face). Off the bat we have Carrey yelling, followed by the couple laughing and joking without the slightest indication that this film is a drama... or a romance even. The trailer ends with Carrey on the frozen pond, screaming, in his silliest voice, "Can you hear *meeee*? I don't *want* this any*mooore*, I wanna call it *off*." The grids appear a final time, before fading to text which reads, "www.lacunainc.com." If we were to expect an ending from the film teased in this trailer, it would be a happy one.

In response to the film's trailer, Sven Mikulec writes for the film blog Cinephilia and Beyond that:

> If you remember 2004 and the time [*Eternal Sunshine*] was released, you might have been misled by the ill-conceived promotional campaign into believing this was a romantic comedy, a happy love story with two exquisite actors, performing in an unexpected collaboration.[77]

In hindsight, the enduring legacy of *Eternal Sunshine* as something of a cult classic suggests otherwise. While the trailer does not represent the inner contents of the film and appears to be "ill-conceived," its more palatable elements are not only carefully constructed, but representative of a trend in early twenty-first century filmmaking.

In charge of the film's marketing and distribution was Focus Features, a small division of the prolific studio heavyweight, Universal Pictures. Founded by James Schamus and David Linde in 2002, Focus was a late addition to the roster of studio specialty divisions which took Hollywood by storm from the mid-1990s to the mid-2000s. Alongside Sony Pictures Classics, Paramount Classics and Paramount Vantage, Picturehouse and Warner Independent Pictures, Fox Searchlight and the Disney-acquired Miramax, Focus Features was established with the goal of releasing a curated selection of lower or mid budget productions with the backing of a major studio label. Their dominance during this time is widely discussed by film scholars, even earning the era its own name: Indiewood. Geoff King, the scholar who coined this term, views the output of these specialty divisions as occupying an intentionally hybrid space between independent and commercial filmmaking: "It is this ability to work on both levels, providing opportunities for the exercise of particular forms of cultural or subcultural capital while also offering wider points of access that marks a characteristic Indiewood blend."[78] Schamus, co-founder of Focus himself said in a diatribe about this convergence of indie and mainstream that independent films at the end of the twentieth century "had succeeded overwhelmingly in entering the mainstream system of commercial exploitation and finance…"[79] Schamus's self-described "rant" about this convergence indicates that Indiewood may have been a negative turn for the authenticity of independent cinema—a "selling out" of the proverbial little guy. But Schamus, King, and all the scholars dissecting this time period are the first to say that Indiewood is not without its merits.

Despite Mikulec's seeming distaste for *Eternal Sunshine's* trailer, there is much to be said for the distributor's hoodwinking of its audience. The chapter dedicated to *Eternal Sunshine* in King's book, *Indiewood, USA: Where Hollywood Meets Independent Cinema*, walks through the deliberate choice on the part of Focus to lean heavily into the tropes of romantic comedy for the film's marketing. King makes particular note of the distributor's Carrey-forward approach to the trailer and posters, arguing that public interest in Carrey's star persona would be piqued if he was framed as a romantic leading man. He quotes the then-head of distribution of Focus in describing their approach as "an extremely unique and aggressive marketing strategy," that assesses the willingness of Americans to "access smart films" and thus uses the commercial accessibility of Carrey to step "outside the confines of the Charlie Kaufman brand."[80]

This is palpable not only from the trailer, which conjures a goofiness that Carrey rarely, if ever, exhibits in the film, but also in the poster, a third of which is taken up by the actor's inquisitive face. For Kaufman and Gondry, as with so many filmmaker-distributor dynamics before them, the process with Focus was a constant push and pull. The original trailer proposed by Focus was of much more conventional stock— with Kaufman and Gondry fighting to remove the familiar baritone of the "*In a world where…*" narrator. "They've shown us the trailer at different stages, and they take our criticism," Kaufman told the *AV Club* during the film's promotional tour, "but they're very selective in what advice they take from us."[81]

The success of Kaufman's previous films like *Being John Malkovich* and *Adaptation*, which speak to audiences through the haze of an energetic, but just barely coherent cinematic psychosis, continues to be something of a marvel to audiences, critics, and film scholars alike. *Eternal Sunshine*, on the other hand, could at least *pretend* to speak the language of the masses.

The raw materials of the film—boy meets girl, they become lovers, lovers have conflict, lovers come back together—was not difficult to package as a romance or rom-com. But of course, the film contains contrasting elements within it, having the structure of a conventional romance but the idiosyncrasies of something more low-fi—cinema verité style dialogue, non-conventional plot, schizophrenic editing, and the paired down performances of A-list actors.

Reviewers and critics in 2004 took note of this hybrid sensibility almost immediately. Jason Perez posited to other cinephiles in the *Home Theater Forum* that since the film was just as "weird, wonderful, and intellectually stimulating" as Kaufman's other films, it would inherently not be "for everyone." However, he concedes, the film "is probably more accessible to a wider audience than Kaufman's previous work, due to its moments of warmth, humanity, and sheer emotional resonance."[82] Roger Ebert articulated in his own review that "[d]espite jumping through the deliberately disorienting hoops of its story, 'Eternal Sunshine' has an emotional center, and that's what makes it work."[83] Anthony Lane, for *The New Yorker*, bemoaned the "meticulous artifice" of other sci-fi movies from the period, using this critique to applaud *Eternal Sunshine* for the fact that "it maintains the beautiful illusion of looking like shit," observing that the film "resembles one of those independent movies which are shot with a borrowed camera for ten thousand dollars."[84] His use of "resembles" here is key. *Eternal Sunshine* is a patina of homemade filmmaking, with its drab mise-en-scène and Kuras's deliberately unsteady hand, that is ultimately a mid-budget film made by a studio subsidiary.

So how is it that I took my date's response that *Eternal Sunshine* was his favorite movie as evidence that he was, in fact, cool? Worthy of a second date? Well, a major pull of Indiewood cinema is its curatorial strategy. What sets its films apart from mainstream Hollywood films is that they have an intrinsic "alternative" appeal, in which "consumers are associating themselves (consciously or unconsciously) with a particular social-cultural domain based on varying degrees of differentiation from mainstream cinema, culture and society."[85] And in tying their own identities to these films, audiences carry them into the future, in turn bestowing on them a degree of longevity. This is how *Eternal Sunshine* now has its cult identity.

Another important aspect of Indiewood films is the

gamble that studios, infamously risk-averse, were allowing for their specialty subsidiaries to take risks on potentially less digestible fare. While the success of a weirdo flick like *Being John Malkovich*, which brought its studio a sizable return given the nature of its premise, was a shock to most, *Eternal Sunshine's* performance was not so exciting. The film was released in March, which took it off the award's notoriously myopic radar, earning it only two nods at the Academy Awards (Kaufman for screenplay and Winslet for Best Actress—Carrey was left out entirely), despite its extreme popularity with critics. And while it was initially released on 1353 screens, compared to a mere 25 for *Malkovich*, it played for only three months.[86] Overall, the movie generated $34 million at the box office, a "less than spectacular return" when marketing costs are considered against the $20 million production budget.

When asked by a reader if he thought *Eternal Sunshine* would have garnered more Oscar buzz if it had been released later in the year, Owen Gleiberman responded in *Entertainment Weekly* with a hypothesis that the film was a bit of a studio experiment when it came to measuring success:

> It couldn't have hurt. *Eternal Sunshine* has, of course, received a handful of awards and nominations, but

there's a general perception in Hollywood that its early-in-the-year release date (March 19) didn't do it any favors. Had the film swapped calendar dates with, say, *Finding Neverland* (Nov. 12), it would now be a lot easier to imagine Jim Carrey looking at a Best Actor nomination instead of Johnny Depp. Given the extraordinary acclaim that has been lavished on *Eternal Sunshine*, it was all but inevitable that the movie would be viewed as a test case—by its studio, Focus Features, and by the rest of the industry— for the question of how an early release date ends up influencing a film's awards chances. The old conventional wisdom was, Hey, it didn't work against *The Silence of the Lambs* (Feb. 14) or *Seabiscuit* (July 25). The new wisdom: Remember *Eternal Sunshine*.[87]

Critical darling or not, by the typical measurements as to whether a movie is successful (did it make money, did it win awards?), the film did a medium job. It seems that the shadowbox of *Eternal Sunshine* carefully put together by Focus had at least partially executed its desired effect—the low-fi nature of the film may not have immediately seduced audiences and awards adjudicators, but over time it would win the hearts of cinephiles.

The uneven footing upon which *Eternal Sunshine* was introduced to the world through its ambiguous status as a cult classic was informed heavily by its Indiewood marketing campaign. And it is perhaps through this wonky convergence of the Indiewood campaign and the loose cult categorization that my friend and I divert so heavily in our associations with the film, with one of us remembering it as basic mainstream fare, and the other as something of an "indie" status symbol. *Eternal Sunshine* continues to evade classification, not a blockbuster, not yet a cult film.

So, to answer the remaining question: was my date "based" or basic for saying *Eternal Sunshine* was his favorite movie?

It doesn't matter. He dumped me.

## Ten: Everybody's Gotta Learn Sometime or The (IM)Potency Of Memory

I often recall words I've heard a hundred times from the Canadian play, *Waiting for the Parade*. The play is presented in the form of a monologue by a woman named Catherine, whose husband Billy has gone missing fighting in World War II. Tipsy and sitting amongst her friends, she warmly recounts once-tense moments from her and Billy's marriage that have been smoothed over by time and distance. For Catherine, a squabble about baseball teams, a fight about religion, or Billy waking her up, rope in hand, and threatening, half-joking, to sink her remains in the river if she doesn't reconcile with him, are now pillars for her fading memories.

I've been engaging in a similar practice recently as memories of my ex become submerged by the passage of time. Life achievements, new friendships, minor heartbreaks, and deaths are detritus in a pool of my once potent emotions, floating about and polluting the water. Painful memories, like Catherine's, become lifeboats for remembering.

Like Joel sitting in the car near the end of the film, driving away from his memory of Montauk and into the blackness of his spotless mind, I ride the plane back to Toronto. Coming home from New York, I am surprised at how little is left of him here. We haven't spoken in several months. "I haven't seen him at all," one friend says to me, "I think he's in Vancouver?" I am surprised that this doesn't feel good. The procedure worked, and now I find myself searching through our painful past. I dig first through my mind, but I can't recall the specifics. I then dig through my bookshelf, and pull out a near-empty journal. I flip to a page titled, "Reasons to move to New York." The first bullet point is his name, and under it I have enumerated various instances in which he hurt me. Reading through the list, I feel a jolt of anger, then a pang of longing. Strangely, I've missed being angry at him. At least then he was in reach. Now, he seems to be vanishing. Sinking to the bottom of the pool.

"Listen," urges Catherine. "If they want to make the Hollywood blockbuster of all time—one of those stories of tragic romance—sure to have every woman in the theatre reaching for her hanky—they should tell the story of a woman—whose husband goes away—but he goes away, one piece at a time. First an arm vanishes. Then a leg. Then his eyes. His hands. His teeth. Finally she can't remember what

*Eternal Sunshine: Auteur*

he looks like—at all. (Pause.) That's what hurts. (Pause.) That's what's—peculiar. (Pause.) Losing him—a little at a time."[88]

Cut to Joel sitting in the Lacuna office, preparing to make his lover go away, bit by bit. Presented with a snow globe he says, "There's a good story behind this actually." Stan interrupts, instructing him to refrain from verbal descriptions: "Just try to focus on the memories"

In his review of *Eternal Sunshine*, A.O Scott explains that in the world of the film, the "perfectly ordinary desire to repress painful memories—to forget the unhappiness of the past and move on—becomes the basis for a kind of self-mutilation that is all the worse for being sold as a form of therapy."[89] Therapy, in the real world, is often used to the opposite effect. In the years I've dedicated to therapy since my breakup, I have learned to practice radical acceptance, to confront and embrace difficult, contradicting truths. My therapist has a favorite gesture—she holds a fist up in the air ("this truth exists") and then the other ("this truth also exists.") She asks me whether both of these can exist at once, to varying degrees of importance.

But the "self-mutilating" therapy offered by Dr. Mierzwiak in the film serves the opposite purpose. It knows the difficulty in confronting these truths, these memories, and preys on our desires to be rid of them altogether. It presents a quick-fix solution. So Scott's negative interpretation invites the question of whether the Lacuna procedure is, indeed, portrayed as detrimental in the film. Is the spotless mind a happy one?

Interestingly, Scott describes this repression of painful memories in *Eternal Sunshine* with the contradicting descriptors of "self-mutilation," and "dispossession." The former inferring that the desire to repress painful memories is done unto oneself, and the latter inferring that these memories are *taken* from you. This concept of "dispossession" comes through most clearly in a scene where Mary, freshly aware of her procedure, tears through the files at the Lacuna office. She comes upon one with her name on it (dated "October 2002") and plays the cassette tape that was stored inside. Dr. Mierzwiak's voice plays, guiding Mary through her memories of him. She discusses liking him immediately because he didn't come onto her, and divulges her fantasies about having his children, before breaking off. Tearily, she says, "Oh Howie, I can't do this." Dr. Mierzwiak softly urges, "We agreed it's for the best Mary." From this exchange, and Mary's subsequent decision to gather all the tapes and mail them back to the clients, it becomes apparent that she has come upon an ethical conundrum.

When we first meet Mary, she comes off as a true

*Eternal Sunshine: Auteur*

professional—dutifully barring Jim from bursting into the office, scolding Stan for his workplace shenanigans, and firmly answering "no" when Joel asks, "this is a hoax, right?"—a question that was not directed to her. Later, she reveals herself to be reverent, almost fanatical, towards the process. Immediately upon entering Joel's home, she and Stan cheer over his bed as she quotes "Blessed are the forgetful." Smoking up, she then goes on in her THC-induced haze to wax poetic about the genius of Howard and his business.

But the youthful ages of Mary and her coworkers in the film is no mistake. After we see Stan rough-housing in the office, he is formally introduced as one of Lacuna's "most experienced and skilled technicians," in a gag where Joel peers into a room in which an agonized woman is strapped to a janky set of machinery as a film projects loudly on the wall beside her. Patrick has no boundaries with the patients, and is presented as an all-around buffoon. And for all of Mary's seeming dedication to Howard and Lacuna, she also drinks, smokes weed and has sex at the site of Joel's procedure. Nevertheless, despite their young, pre-cynical spirits, Mary, especially, is a force for remembering. The resilience of her love is proof that Dr. Mierzwiak's technology is fallible.

Mary's despair upon finding out that her memories have

been erased also suggests that the process may not be as altruistic as it purports to be. Mierzwiak assures Mary that erasure was her choice to make: "You wanted the procedure. You wanted it done so you could get past..." But his inability to articulate just what exactly Mary wanted to get past, and his persuasive, "we agreed it's for the best," leaves one to infer that Mary may have been coerced into the procedure for the sake of Howard's reputation. Mary's final moment of realization may in part stem from a feeling that she's been preyed upon. In the moment, Mary's agony over Dr. Mierzwiak may have pushed her to want the procedure, as the impulse to repress painful memories is a "perfectly ordinary desire." However, the procedure leaves her vulnerable to the people around her, people who possess information about Mary of which she herself has been dispossessed. Howard's preying on perfectly ordinary impulses becomes doubly insidious when it's considered in this context—profiting off extreme but fleeting human emotions by repackaging the eradication of these base, but perhaps necessary, desires "as a form of therapy." Ultimately, Mary is a casualty of convenience.

Near the end of the film, Mary is packing her belongings into the trunk of her car when Stan breathily apprehends her in a final bid to salvage their relationship. He promises Mary that he was not aware of her procedure (given his chastising of Patrick earlier in the film, I am inclined to believe him), and only vaguely suspected her affair with Howard when he saw the two of them talking together a long time before. "How'd I look?" asks Mary. Stan sighs and pauses to think. "You looked happy... happy with a secret." "And after that?" Stan evades the question, his avoidance pregnant with the assumption that Mary was, in fact, less happy after her procedure. Whether or not there is truth to this assumption, Mary's despair over this revelation is palpable—so palpable that it has driven her to quit her job and forsake the career of her boss and former lover. Mary's breaking free of Lacuna is not liberating or celebratory, but somewhat bittersweet. Mary is not happy, but she will be.

Now, what about Clementine?

*Eternal Sunshine* is designed for repeat viewings. And the train sequence in particular is one that appears completely different with each new watch. On my latest viewing, it became apparent to me that I had been misreading Clementine's behavior all these years. On an initial viewing of this sequence when Joel and Clementine meet for the second "first time" on the train, Clementine comes off as quirky, if not a bit terse. She is blunt, and drives the conversation into random, abrupt tangents—but to the viewer and to Joel this is exciting.

However, on my latest viewing, Clementine came across as very erratic. Self-deprecating about her hair she says, "I apply my personality in a paste," and Joel affirms, "I doubt that very much." Clementine's disposition then changes quickly, "Well you don't know me so… you don't know, do you?" Joel is confused, "I was just trying to be nice." In these exchanges, Clementine is overly reactive and short with Joel. Odd behavior towards someone she has "just met."

In another instance, Joel refers to Clementine as "nice," which she does not take kindly to. This may have unearthed some deep-seated leftover feelings from their relationship, with Joel being so concerned with niceties and villainizing Clementine for minor social transgressions. "I don't need nice. I don't need myself to be it and I don't need anybody else to be it at me." Very quickly, she acquiesces, apologizing and sighing deeply, before admitting, "I'm a little out of sorts today."

The music is very loud in this sequence, with the actors' voices occasionally drowned out by the sporadic honking of brass instruments. The silliness of this musical arrangement could, on an initial viewing, appear to highlight the quirkiness of Clementine's demeanor as it collides with Joel's. But upon multiple viewings, it mostly serves to emphasize the bizarreness of their encounter. Clementine's behavior is not so much endearing as it is confused and disjointed. She assures Joel that, while she had a strong reaction to the word nice, she actually thinks Joel is quite nice: "I can't tell from one moment to the next what I'm gonna like, but right now I'm glad you are." Again, Clementine's inability to decide on someone reads at first as characteristic of the manic pixie, a woman who lives from moment to moment. But with the knowledge that Clementine has already undergone the memory removal procedure, her disorientation is tragic. Her alleged "quirks" are not endearing because they aren't so much a facet of her personality, as they are indicative of someone who has suffered some sort of trauma.

If there are other clear indications of Clementine's post-procedure state of mind, it is in the moment where Mary is lying in bed with Stan and muses that, "Howard makes it all go away." From here, the scene immediately cuts to Clementine letting Patrick, who has just left Joel's, into her apartment. Clementine looks tear-stricken. Patrick follows her into the apartment and asks her what's going on. "I don't know. I don't know. I'm lost. I'm scared, I feel like I'm disappearing. My skin's coming off. I'm getting old! Nothing makes any sense to me." Driving herself into a frenzy, she repeats this final phrase, "nothing makes any sense" again and again. Patrick, knowing very well what's going on, simply chuckles.

It is easy to attribute Joel's disquieting journey through his memories to the fact that his procedure has been botched. But Clementine's discombobulation suggests that the procedure is, even in its proper full capacity, quite scary, according to Matt Mansfield of *Dazed*:

> ...the film presents the idea of therapeutic memory erasure as a bad thing: Kaufman has the procedure's inventor and practitioner describe it as a form of "brain damage", while Gondry's presentation of the subconscious effect of the treatment is as nightmarish and traumatic as possible from a visual standpoint.[90]

The only times post-procedure Clementine is brought out of her terror is when she is either with Joel, or reminded of him. To soothe her frenzy, Patrick appropriates her memories of Joel. For example, he gives her a "gift" for Valentine's Day—a gift he stole from Joel. "What is it?" she asks, not catching onto the bizarreness of the following response: "I don't know, open it!" It turns out to be a necklace, which is just Clementine's taste! She thanks him and he gives her a kiss, and her paranoia resurfaces. She casts Patrick a suspicious look. The gift was Joel, the kiss was not. Clem is ambivalent towards Patrick. And it becomes apparent as the film goes on that her interest in him is a result of this Joel-shaped mask he wears—a sign that perhaps she and Joel really are meant to be or, at the very least, worth another try.

Realizations like this are underscored by the inclusion of Joel's childhood memories. When he and Clementine are sitting on the couch, Clem presents him with an idea: "The eraser guys are coming here, so what if you take me somewhere else? Somewhere I don't belong. And we hide there till morning?" Where *is* a memory where Clementine would not belong?

In Joel's childhood of course, long before they met.

In typical Gondry fashion, the transition to childhood has an analog sensibility to it. Rain begins to pour in the living room, and Joel giddily ducks for cover under a table. Now we enter the childhood sequence.

What is stark about these memories is that they are not exactly happy. The first is little Joel cowering from the rain. Another is him hiding under the kitchen table, whining for his busy mother to pay attention to him. Another one that is "really buried," is a teenage Joel masturbating and being caught by his mother. This one takes him right off the map, forcing Dr. Mierzwiak to stay back and look for him.

Finally, we land on a scene that always brings me to tears. Now, we're "somewhere *really* buried." Little Joel, adorned with a red cape and kneeling before a red wagon, surrounded by a group of other little boys. Inside the wagon is a dead bird. A little blonde girl in cowboy gear, likely a younger Clementine (who has been transported into this memory) watches from the sidelines with a look of disgust. Carrey's voice is heard insisting, "I'll do it later!" But little Joel buckles under the pressure and begins to bludgeon the bird with a hammer. Everyone falls silent, and little Clementine marches over and grabs little Joel by the hand. A shot of a bird in a nearby tree flying away, then cut back to an adult Joel and Clementine, wearing the same childlike costumes. Joel is now crying in shame, and Clementine gives the boys a stern look before pulling him away.

What the viewer notices first is the music, which begins to play as Joel and Clementine walk away. Whatever discomfort we feel from the mutilation of the bird, or the silliness of Carrey and Winslet acting like children, is eclipsed by delicate, melancholic notes from a piano. Even as an adult Joel is physically overpowered by what is clearly his childhood bully, even as he oafishly yells "Stupid!" at them in a last-ditch effort to regain his dignity, we are overtaken by the poignancy of this moment. Washed in cold blue hues, this is undoubtedly a very painful memory for Joel. "I feel so ashamed," Joel says in voiceover. Little Clementine pats him on the back, reassuring him, "It's okay! You were a little kid." The music, choppy editing, and floating words create a tapestry of contradicting emotions. The scene is somber and uncomfortable, but its formal elements tell us to search for its beauty. What we see is not matched by what we feel. It is a scene that neatly encapsulates the film's overarching message. Despite the fact that Clementine doesn't belong to this memory, it emphasizes her and Joel's need to remember each other. It's as though Joel cannot fathom a time in which Clementine wasn't present in his life. Each time I watch this scene, I'm overcome by a strong sensation of grief. I miss being in sync with another person, against the rest of the world.

The childhood sequences signal a turning point in the film. In being forced to confront them, Joel begins to discover joy in what were once unhappy memories. James Bowman phrases it well, arguing that *Eternal Sunshine* is "persuasive that we have to hang on to the bad memories as well as the good. But the [...] film also goes on to suggest that the bad ones are somehow included in the good ones and are redeemed by them."[91]

As the memories of my ex fade, I cling to one in particular. We were on a day trip to Sintra, the colorful, palace-laden town about thirty minutes outside of Lisbon, Portugal. By this point, weeks of heavy drinking and sleep deprivation had caught up to me, and I was experiencing near-debilitating anxiety. Things came to a head while we were sitting in a restaurant eating lunch and, losing complete control, I ran to the bathroom to throw up. Up until then, I had not voiced to him what was happening with me. But now that things had turned physical, I confessed, "I'm not okay right now." He gave me a big hug, and told me that we didn't need to take the bus up the mountain to Pena Palace. We could just walk up slowly instead and get some fresh air. Knowing this was almost an hour-long walk, I knew how much he was inconveniencing himself.

As we walked, and I divulged the torturous thoughts that had been running through my mind over the past two weeks, I felt the anxiety leave my body. It's doubtful that he remembers this and it's by no means a happy memory, but it was formative both for myself and for our relationship.

A similar moment occurs in the film, when Joel officially decides he no longer wants to go through with the procedure. Lying in bed, he comforts Clementine, who is crying. Again, she references childhood: "Sometimes I think people don't understand how lonely it is to be a kid. Like you don't matter." She recounts to him a memory from when she was eight, and she yelled at her ugly doll to "just be prettier." "It's weird," she says, "like if I could transform her, I could change too." A hopeful tune builds and Clementine gives a sad smile.

Joel has been watching her with a look of understanding, maybe a growing realization that he loves her. He rolls over and kisses her, as she pleads with him to "never leave." The scene until this point has been lit with soft yellows but then changes to the dark flash-lighting. Slipping away and clawing at the bedsheets, this is the first time we hear Joel ask, "Please let me keep this one." Clementine disappears.

It takes a bereaved mind to notice that many of Joel's memories are formative, in spite of their dark context. The goal of grief is not to overcome it, but to embrace it. For we are nothing if not a web of memories. Without memories, we are Catherine, flailing in the dark. We are Clementine, frantic and confused. We are Mary, palpably less happy. As Roger Ebert writes in his review, "The insight of 'Eternal Sunshine' is that, at the end of the day, our memories are all we really have, and when they're gone, we're gone."[92] Wizened now, we come to the conclusion, as we stare at the white screen, that there is no bliss in the spotless mind. There is only nothing.

About three months after our break-up, my ex said something that I will never forget. At the time, it was obvious to me and everyone close to him that he was floundering in grief and having trouble finding reprieve. But on the phone one day, he relayed to me some wisdom he had recently learned from a friend—that while this moment was abjectly painful, it was important not to push it away: "When else are we going to feel emotions like this again? It's kind of beautiful." I agreed. My tears were a testament to the love I had for him, my first love, and a love I am still unsure I will ever find again—but one that I hold out hope for.

I've since repeated this wisdom to friends experiencing their own romantic grief. One day we will be older and these feelings will be behind us. Just as I now find comfort in the humiliation of my adolescent years, I know that in the future I will look back on this break-up and long to feel so strongly again.

Few of Joel's fondest memories are perfectly happy.

*Eternal Sunshine: Auteur*

Neither are mine. Joel recalling that Clementine was wearing an orange sweatshirt when they first met, one he would "hate eventually." Us, blackout drunk and break-dancing in a hotel room, shortly before I threw up on him (again). Joel telling Clementine that he left her alone in Montauk when they first met, because, "You said 'so go' with such disdain, you know?" Me, crying on the phone, selfishly pleading with him to move back to Montreal.

On Boxing Day, he said to me, "I feel like I made your life terrible."

He didn't. We had a beautiful relationship, an enviable one even. Two people who made each other laugh, and walked the sordid uphill battle of our early twenties together. We were best friends in love. Mundanely pushed apart by age, circumstance, location, and eventually, ourselves.

By the end of our relationship, we were barely functioning, our issues ballooning into something too great for either of us to ignore. We ended things for reasons we probably now forget, and promised we would stay in each other's lives.

Now, we no longer speak.

But the reason I refuse to forget him is because I would not be who I am today without him. Cliches abound, every memory *is* a piece of me.

Joel and Clementine's decisions to forget are reactionary and impulsive. They are too quick to snip the strip. They haven't had the necessary time and distance to miss each other, to embrace their memories. And so *Eternal Sunshine* starts with the bad and ends with the good, reminding us why they were together in the first place. A compelling argument for why they should "give it another go around." Clem puts her arms around him in the bookstore. "Remember me. Try your best. Maybe we can!"

With time, I realize that my viewings of the film before and after my break-up are not so different. *Eternal Sunshine* is itself a memory, an elixir of feelings with good and bad mixed in. I drank this elixir a long time ago to remind myself of our love. Later, I drank it to confront my pain. These two things are the same. Grief is not a science. There is no real answer.

In *Giovanni's Room*, James Baldwin's grief-ridden protagonist ponders the impossibility of memory:

> ...life only offers the choice of remembering the garden or forgetting it. Either, or: it takes strength to remember, it takes another kind of strength to forget, it takes a hero to do both. People who remember court madness through pain, the pain of the perpetually

recurring death of their innocence; people who forget court another kind of madness, the madness of the denial of pain and the hatred of innocence; and the world is mostly divided between madmen who remember and madmen who forget. Heroes are rare.[93]

I'd like to think there's something hideously, maybe even embarrassingly heroic about the pain I have put myself through over these past few years. I am courting the madness of keeping alive a series of memories that sometimes wake me up in the middle of the night, crying, and sometimes push me forward through life. Some see the white screen as cowardly, I see a terrible heroism. I see a bright, shining, beautiful grief.

About two months after our breakup, my ex asked me if I saw us getting back together. I said, "I don't know." I still wonder whether this is what pushed him away, why he no longer wants to know me. I still don't know if we're Joel and Clementine, whether we're meant to find each other on the beach. But I do know I miss him. I don't have him anymore, but I have my memories, and that has to be enough. As Jim Carrey says:

These days everybody expects that fairy tale [that]

you're going to be together forever with somebody and I don't really subscribe to that. I'd love that to happen if that happened, but 10 years is enough. 10 years is a good thing with somebody, I think. It's a nice thing. A lot of good love can happen in 10 years.[94]

We can't give it another go around, and I'm sure neither of us would want to. But the light I shine for him has not gone out. And I continue to hope that one day he will see it and re-enter my life, however that may look.

For now, I watch *Eternal Sunshine* to remember.

Thank you to Allyson Shap, for your big beautiful brain.

## NOTES

1. Morris, Craig E. and Christoph Reiber. "Frequency, intensity and expression of post-relationship grief." *EvoS Journal* (2011), 2.

2. Verhallen et al, "Romantic relationship breakup: An experimental model to study effects of stress on depression (-like) symptoms," *PLoS ONE* 14(5): e0217320. https://doi.org/10.1371/journal.pone.0217320, 10.

3. Kenneth J. Doka, *Disenfranchised Grief: Recognizing Hidden Sorrow* (Lexington: Lexington Books, 1989), 3.

4. Ibid.

5. Joan Didion, *The Year of Magical Thinking*, (New York: Knopf, 2005), 99.

6. Didion, 44.

7. Charles Dickens, *Nicholas Nickleby*, (United States: ReadHowYouWant.com, Limited, 1898), 123.

8. Lynn Hirschberg, "Le Romantique," *New York Times*, Sept 17, 2006, https://www.nytimes.com/2006/09/17/magazine/le-romantique.html.

9. Matt Mansfield, "Ten Years of *Eternal Sunshine of the Spotless Mind*," *Dazed*, March 13, 2014, https://www.dazeddigital.com/artsandculture/article/19247/1/a-secret-history-of-michel-gondry.

10. A. O. Scott, "Charlie Kaufman's Critique of Pure Comedy," *New York Times*, April 4, 2004, https://www.nytimes.com/2004/04/04/arts/film-charlie-kaufman-s-critique-of-pure-comedy.html.

11. David Ehrlich, "Charlie Kaufman Reflects On His Career: 'I Feel Like I F*cking Blew It,'" *IndieWire*, July 12, 2016, https://www.indiewire.com/features/interviews/charlie-kaufman-interview-anomalisa-synecdoche-adaptation-1201702465/.

12. Michael Sragow, "Being Charlie Kaufman," *Salon*, November 11, 1999, https://www.salon.com/1999/11/11/kaufman/.

13. Neil McGlone, "From Pen to Screen: An Interview with Charlie Kaufman," *Criterion*, August 9, 2016, https://www.criterion.com/current/posts/4177-from-pen-to-screen-an-interview-with-charlie-kaufman?srsltid=AfmBOoqcucpIuzIpKkXIVWzAlmqwi9QqlVj96QfjaEhHrSb-If_E7IO0.

14. Robert Hughes, "Art: Modernism's Patriarch," *Time*, June 10, 1996, https://time.com/archive/6729137/art-modernisms-patriarch/.

15. Ehrlich

16. Jon Baskin, "Can Charlie Kaufman Get Out of His Head?" *The New Yorker*. August 12, 2020, https://www.newyorker.com/books/under-review/can-charlie-kaufman-get-out-of-his-head.

17. Ibid.

18. David S. Cohen, "From Script to Screen: 'Eternal Sunshine Of The Spotless Mind'," *Script Magazine*, February 17, 2016. https://scriptmag.com/features/

script-screen-eternal-sunshine-of-the-spotless-mind.

19. "Charlie Kaufman on his latest film & why "movies are dead,""WGA West, 2008, 9 min., 2 sec., https://www.youtube.com/watch?v=oxps3oouNiQ&ab_channel=WGAWest.

20. Sragow

21. Adam Sternbergh, "Charlie Kaufman," *Vulture*, December 16, 2015. https://www.vulture.com/2015/12/charlie-kaufman-anomaslisa-c-v-r.html.

22. David LaRocca, *The Philosophy of Charlie Kaufman*, (Lexington: University Press of Kentucky, 2011), 8.

23. LaRocca, 14.

24. Ibid.

25. Cohen

26. NTSC Region 1, "Michel Gondry, Chris Cunningham & Spike Jonze Q & A" Aidan Duffy, 2017, 9 min., twenty-four seconds., https://www.youtube.com/watch?v=QuLboDic6As&t=2s&ab_channel=AidanDuffy.

27. Sven Schumann and Johannes Bonke, "Michel Gondry: I Believe in Utopia," *The Talks*, June 27, 2011, https://the-talks.com/interview/michel-gondry/.

28. "Michel Gondry (Kidding) | Production Value | Title Designer/Director", Deadline Hollywood, 2020, 3 min., forty-two seconds., https://www.youtube.com/watch?v=4ue8t6FalaU&ab_channel=DeadlineHollywood.

29. Hirschberg, "Le Romantique".

30. Nathan Rabin,"Undomesticated Case File#148:Human Nature," *AV Club*, October 14, 2009, https://www.avclub.com/undomesticated-case-file-148-human-nature-1798218053.

31. Scott Tobias, "Michel Gondry & Charlie Kaufman," *AV Club*, March 17, 2004, https://www.avclub.com/

michel-gondry-charlie-kaufman-1798208337.

32. Hirschberg, "Le Romantique".

33. Schumann and Bonke.

34. Michel Gondry, "Forward by Michel Gondry" in *Eternal Sunshine of the Spotless Mind*, ed. Christopher Grau, (New York: Routledge, 2009).

35. Gondry, "Forward".

36. Ibid.

37. Ibid.

38. Hirschberg, "Le Romantique".

39. Mansfield.

40. Gondry, "Forward".

41. James Bowman, "Memory and the Movies," *The New Atlantis*, No. 5 (Spring 2004), 85.

42. John Pavlus, "Forget Me Not: Eternal Sunshine of the Spotless Mind" *American Cinematographer*, April 24, 2020, https://theasc.com/articles/forget-me-not-eternal-sunshine-of-the-spotless-mind.

43. Pavlus.

44. Ibid.

45. Ibid.

46. Tobias.

47. Pavlus.

48. Yohana Desta, "Mind Games and Broken Hearts: Jim Carrey and Michel Gondry on Making Eternal Sunshine," *Vanity Fair*, March 19, 2019, https://www.vanityfair.com/hollywood/2019/03/eternal-sunshine-of-the-spotless-mind-anniversary-jim-carrey-michel-gondry?srsltid=AfmBOoo7cn-HUMK3oNEe_cZdURTDwJ9eMM3ZkrfH2-Dqe2q21X-Ldj3IvX.

49. Pavlus

50. Schumann and Bonke.

51. Ibid.

52. Hirschberg.

53. "Kate Winslet and Michel Gondry (*Eternal Sunshine of the Spotless Mind*)" Bernard Black, June 11, 2017, fourteen min., twenty-four sec., https://www.youtube.com/watch?v=g9R61PLRAIk&ab_channel=BernardBlack.

54. Hirschberg.

55. "Kate Winslet and Michel Gondry."

56. "Jim Carrey: Characters, Comedy, and Existence: TIFF Long Take," TIFF Originals, October 23, 2017, twenty-six min., forty-six sec., https://www.youtube.com/watch?v=LMnrH1CN4oc&ab_channel=TIFFOriginals.

57. Dan Zak, "Interview: Jim Carrey, Kate Winslet and cast of 'Eternal Sunshine'," *The Eagle*, March 18, 2004, https://www.theeagleonline.com/article/2004/03/interview-jim-carrey-kate-winslet-and-cast-of-eternal-sunshine.

58. Rebecca Murray, "Jim Carrey on "Eternal Sunshine of the Spotless Mind," Memories, & Michel Gondry" Live About, May 24, 2019, https://www.liveabout.com/jim-carrey-on-eternal-sunshine-of-the-spotless-mind-2419275.

59. Rabin.

60. "Eternal Sunshine of the Spotless Mind - Kate Winslet & Michel Gondry Interview," *Charlie Rose* (2004)

61. Zak.

62. Desta.

63. "Behind The Scenes | *Eternal Sunshine of the Spotless Mind* (2004)" Industria Movies, one min., fifty-four sec., https://www.youtube.com/

watch?v=NRGdKbwlsBM&ab_channel=IndustriaMovies.

64. Murray.

65. Desta.

66. Tobias.

67. Schumann and Bonke.

68. Elena Gorfinkel, "Cult Film or Cinephilia by Any Other Name," *Cinéaste*, 34, No. 1 (Winter 2008), 35.

69. Gorfinkel, 38.

70. Briggs et al, "Cult Cinema: A Critical Symposium," *Cinéaste*, Vol. 34, No. 1 (Winter 2008), 44.

71. Briggs et al, 44.

72. Ibid.

73. Briggs et al, 46.

74. Briggs et al, 44.

75. Tobias.

76. Umberto Eco, "Casablanca": Cult Movies and Intertextual Collage," *SubStance*, 4, No. 2, (1985), 4.

77. Mikulec.

78. Geoff King, *Indiewood, USA Where Hollywood meets Independent Cinema*, (New York: I.B.Tauris & Co, 2009), 86.

79. James Schamus, "A Rant" in *The End of Cinema As We Know It : American Film in the Nineties*, ed. John Lewis (London : Pluto Press, 2002), p. 254.

80. King, 83.

81. Tobias.

82. Todd McCarthy, "Eternal Sunshine of the Spotless Mind," *Variety*, March 11, 2004, https://variety.com/2004/film/awards/eternal-sunshine-of-the-spotless-mind-2-1200534526/.

83. Roger Ebert, "Eternal Sunshine of the Spotless Mind"

rogerebert.com, March 19, 2004, https://www.rogerebert.com/reviews/eternal-sunshine-of-the-spotless-mind-2004.

84. Anthony Lane, "Don't Look Back: Eternal Sunshine of the Spotless Mind," *The New Yorker*, March 14, 2004, https://www.newyorker.com/magazine/2004/03/22/dont-look-back

85. King, 12.

86. King, 82.

87. Owen Gleiberman, "Why did "Eternal Sunshine" get overlooked for awards?" *Entertainment Weekly*, February 21, 2005, https://ew.com/article/2005/02/21/why-did-eternal-sunshine-get-overlooked-awards/#:~:text=Eternal%20Sunshine%20has%2C%20of%20course,say%2C%20Finding%20Neverland%20(Nov.

88. John Murrell, *Waiting for the Parade*, (Calgary: Concord Theatricals, 1977).

89. Scott.

90. Mansfield.

91. Bowman, 90.

92. Roger Ebert, "Eternal Sunshine of the Spotless Mind" rogerebert.com (March 19, 2004).

93. James Baldwin, *Giovanni's Room*, (New York: Dial Press N.Y, 1956), 25.

94. Murray.

www.ingramcontent.com/pod-product-compliance
Lightning Source LLC
Jackson TN
JSHW080004130525
84332JS00004B/290